6 —
H⁶

THE
EXPEDITION COOKBOOK

THE EXPEDITION COOKBOOK

CAROLYN GUNN

CHOCKSTONE PRESS
Denver, Colorado
CORDEE
Leicester
1988

Published and distributed in North America by
Chockstone Press, Inc.
526 Franklin Street
Denver, Colorado 80218
(303) 377-1970

ISBN 0-934641-08-0

Published simultaneously in Great Britain by
CORDEE
3a De Montfort Street
Leicester LE1 7HD
Great Britain

ISBN 0-904405-69-9

Cover photo by Michael Kennedy

Table of Contents

To the memory of my father, the first outdoorsman
I knew and the man who taught me to love the
wilderness

Preface

"Necessity is the mother of invention."

Plato
THE REPUBLIC

*L*OOKING BACK AT the time when I was first asked to accompany a large expedition as cook and basecamp manager, I now realize I had no idea what was involved. I could cook well outdoors, but I had very little experience in the other numerous skills needed to plan meals, shop, pack and ship the food and organize it into porter and animal loads and distribute those loads to the necessary camps. Likewise, I was ill-prepared for the myriad odd jobs that everyone looks to the cook to perform and no inkling of all the little tasks and problems that arise for which only experience can provide answers.

Knowing many others were probably in a similar situation, I set about organizing the things I was learning into a form that could benefit others, as well as myself.

The result is this book. It is mainly addressed to those mounting any type of expedition, whether it be for climbing in the Himalayas, for scientific research in polar regions, or for any group entering the backcountry for any length of time.

Additionally, I have designed the book so it will be helpful for outdoor skills schools and teachers, and for experiential education programs.

Also, and never least in my mind as I prepared the manuscript, this book is for the individual who may only hike or climb on the weekends; hopefully, the necessary encumbrances of cooking and camplife can be overcome by knowledge gained from this book.

Although I have tried to be as complete and accurate as possible with my treatment of the material covered, it is, by nature of the subject, only a partial coverage of the extensive theme of "camp cooking". Any camper develops his own likes and dislikes, opinions, and favorite ways of doing things. Therefore, this book is a presentation of my opinions and outdoor philosophies, tempered by experience and research, which hopefully closely approaches the best way.

In preparing this book I have learned many things, and I pass this knowledge to the reader with the firm hope that it makes his interaction with the environment easier and richer.

Notes About the Book

- The pronouns "he" and "his" are used throughout the text for simplicity and in no way should be construed that "her" and "hers" are not equal.
- Most linear, volume and weight measurements are presented in the metric system. However, because of familiarity with avoirdupois weight used for cooking measurements, difficulty in converting recipes to metric measures and lack of adequate metric cooking utensils, recipes are in conventional measurements.
- A summary is included at the end of certain chapters in order to point out salient features presented throughout the chapter.
- The listing of any products in this book is not an endorsement or sanction of that product, but rather a means by which to inform the reader of options available to suit his specific needs.

Chapter 1

Introduction

We may live without poetry, music and art;
We may live without conscience, and live without heart;
We may live without friends, we may live without books;
But civilized man cannot live without cooks.

Edward Robert Bulwer, Earl of Lytton
LUCILE

P LANNING ANY ASPECT of a large expedition or mountaineering trip can be quite a feat, but few things are as frustrating as planning the food. Not only do amounts, costs, weight and transport have to be considered, but individual preferences among the group members can present almost insurmountable problems. Since the ultimate goal is to provide adequate nutrition in less than favorable conditions (at altitude, to people with waning appetites) their individual prejudices cannot be taken lightly. There must be something for everybody.

Therefore, before pulling foods indiscriminately off the grocer's shelves, much thought must be given to the process of planning the food for a large trip. These thoughts should begin with an understanding of nutrition and an accounting for the numbers of individuals and the duration of the trip.

Thus, in a logical, albeit time consuming manner, can one plan and provide adequate nutrition without unnecessary redundancy of some foods, lack of other foods, or tedium of an unvaried menu.

Another main consideration in planning the food for a large trip – particularly a siege-type Himalayan climb – is the "pyramid effect", where allowances must be made for food which will be consumed while getting other necessary food and equipment to the furthest camps.

While procuring food supplies, one must keep in mind subsequent packing, shipping and portering of these items, as this may determine the form in which the food is bought.

In backcountry situations, an understanding of stoves, fuels, cooking equipment and alteration of cooking processes by high altitude is an integral part of the food preparation process.

Although camp hygiene is not a subject of cookery *per se*, it is an essential part of preparing healthful meals.

Throughout the pages of this book are guidelines for all of the above-mentioned aspects of expedition and mountaineering cookery. With this information, planning and procuring as well as shipping and preparing food in the backcountry can be an easier, more rewarding experience.

Chapter 2
A Knowledge of Nutrition

"Willi and I attacked the problem of eating with a stubborn determination . . . . As long as there was food, we ate. We would neatly clean the leftovers of those whose appetites were jading, and we competed even in this. In due course we would stagger distended to our tents and sit dazed and breathless on our sleeping bags, barely able to bend over and untie our boots."

Thomas F. Hornbein
EVEREST: THE WEST RIDGE

CARBOHYDRATES, FATS, PROTEINS, vitamins, minerals and water are the six nutrients. Each nutrient has its own specific functions and relationships to the body, but no nutrient acts independently of other nutrients. The necessary amounts of these nutrients vary slightly from one individual to another based on age, sex, weight, environment, activity level, genetic makeup and health status.[1]

Nutrient composition is influenced by the inherent characteristics and environmental conditions of the plant or animal from which it is derived. The method of storage, handling, processing and cooking also has an effect on the nutitrional value of the food. For example, highly processed foods such as bleached flour, polished rice and refined sugar are low in vitamins, minerals and cellulose.[1]

In order for a diet to be balanced, adequate amounts and ratios of the six nutrients are necessary. Under varying conditions of environment and exercise, the ratios of fats, proteins and carbohydrates can be rearranged to produce an optimally balanced diet.[2]

Carbohydrates

Carbohydrates are the chief source of energy for all body functions and supply energy in an easily absorbed and metabolizable form. In addition, carbohydrates regulate protein and fat metabolism, and carbohydrates are necessary for the breakdown of fat within the liver. Principle carbohydrates in food are in the form of sugars, starches and cellulose, the latter being indigestable by humans. Simple sugars such as table sugar, honey and fruit sugars are easily digested. Starches such as grains require enzymatic action in order to be broken down into simple sugars for digestion. Cellulose in its indigestable form provides bulk in the diet which aids intestinal action and elimination. Excess glucose (blood sugar) produced by digestion is converted to a larger molecule, glycogen, and stored in liver and muscle; further excess is converted to fat and stored as energy reserves. When fat reserves are reconverted to glucose to be used for body fuel, weight loss results. Carbohydrates produce a feeling of "instant energy" because they cause a sudden rise in the blood sugar level, but this level drops again rapidly, creating a rebound feeling of fatigue and a craving for more sweets.[1] Candy, sugar, pastries, cereals, legumes, fruits, vegetables and milk are sources of carbohydrates. As a general rule, carbohydrates should provide 50% of the daily caloric intake. Carbohydrates have an energy value of 4.0 kilocalories/gram.[2]

Fats

Fats are the most concentrated source of energy in the diet and provide a sustained energy source. Fats also are required for the absorption of the fat soluble vitamins A, D, E, and K. Meals high in fat prolong the process of digestion and create a long lasting feeling of fullness after a meal.[1] Fat metabolism, however, is inefficient and requires three to four times more oxygen for metabolism than required by carbohydrates. Five times more energy is needed to convert fats into body fuels than carbohydrates.[3] Fats are made of saturated and unsaturated fatty acids. Saturated fatty acids, except for coconut oil, come from animal sources and usually are firm at room temperature. Unsaturated fatty acids are usually liquid at room temperture and are derived from vegetable sources. Some vegetable shortening products and margarines have been processed so they are firm at room temperature, but this does not alter their basic unsaturated nature. Certain fatty acids are "essential" because the body cannot manufacture them and they must be supplied in the diet. Sources of fats are meats, butter and milk fat products, eggs, nuts and vegetable oils and spreads. Nutritionists suggest fat should provide 25 to 30% of the daily caloric intake.[1] Fats have an energy value of 9.0 kilocalories/gram.[2]

Proteins

Dietary protein is used as a sustained source of heat and energy in the body. Protein is also the major source of building material for the body, for enzymes and antibodies, and it is essential in regulation of the blood clotting mechanism. When sufficient fats and carbohydrates are present in the diet, the use of protein for energy is spared. Excess protein not used for energy is converted by the liver and stored as fat in the body. Digestion of proteins results in production of amino acids which are then used as building blocks of body protein. Of the 22 amino acids needed to make human protein, all but eight are produced in the body. The remaining eight amino acids are called "essential amino acids" because it is essential that they are provided by the diet. Foods containing all of the essential amino acids are called complete proteins and come from most meats, dairy products and eggs. Incomplete proteins are lacking in one or more essential amino acids. Cereals, legumes, vegetables and fruits are incomplete protein sources but can be made complete by combining with foods adequate in the missing amino acids. The National Research Council (NRC) recommends an intake of 0.92 grams of protein/day/kilogram of body weight (or, body weight in pounds divided by 2 equals an estimate of the grams of protein required per day).[1] Protein needs of an active person, however, can be as high as 1.5 grams of protein/day/kilogram of body weight. Ten to 15% of daily caloric intake at altitude should be from protein. Too high a level of protein in the diet may enhance dehydration, as urea, a by-product of protein metabolism, requires a certain volume of water to be excreted with it in the urine.[4] Sources of proteins include meat, fish, poultry, legumes, seeds and nuts, cheese and dairy products, eggs and whole grains. Proteins should constitute 20 to 25% of the daily caloric intake. Proteins have an energy value of 4.0 kilocalories/gram.[2]

Vitamins

Vitamins are usually supplied in ordinary balanced diets, especially those containing fresh fruits and vegetables, milk and meats.[2] Vitamins are not components of body structures, but aid in the building of those structures. In most instances, the body cannot produce vitamins, and they or their precursors must be supplied in the diet.[1] On extended expeditions, the combination of poorly balanced diets, the use of processed, dried foods, and lack of fresh meats, fruits and vegetables can result in vitamin deficiency. Therefore, vitamin supplementation is an easy, inexpensive way to insure proper vitamin intake.[2] Requirements of vitamins under such conditions are unknown, but twice the recommended daily allowance is suggested.[3] Vitamins taken in excess of the amount utilized in the metabolic processes are either excreted or stored in the body. Excessive ingestion of some vitamins may result in toxicity. Some vitamins such as vitamin C are unstable and are sensititve to oxidation by heat, light and air and can decrease the vitamin content of foods.[1]

Minerals

Minerals are nutrients that must be supplied by the diet. They are actual constituents of many body tissues and are very important in the metabolic processes of the body. In most instances, a diet supplying adequate protein and energy needs also supplies adequate minerals.[1] Like vitamins, however, inadequate mineral intake may result from a poor diet encountered on an expedition, and twice the recommended daily allowance of mineral supplementation may be required.[3] Women have been found to have significantly higher hemoglobin levels when supplemental iron was given to support altitude-induced increase in red blood cell production, but this was not true for men.[5] Evidence for additional iron to support red cell production at altitude is conflicting.[6]

Water

Although not generally thought of as a nutrient, water is absolutely essential to life, and proper daily intake demands strict attention. Plain water, as well as soup, tea, coffee, fruit juices and other liquids taken in the course of the day and at meals help increase daily water consumption and help maintain hydration. Climatic conditions and levels of physical exertion greatly affect the amount of necessary daily water intake.

ENERGY REQUIREMENTS

A "small" calorie or gram calorie (abbreviated cal) is the amount of energy needed to raise the temperature of 1 gram of water 1°c. A "large" calorie is also termed a kilogram calorie or kilocalorie (abbreciated Cal or Kcal) and is a unit of food calculation equivalent to 1,000 small calories. It is the amount of energy needed to raise the temperature of 1 kilogram of water 1°c. The basal metabolism uses about 1 kilocalorie per kilogram of body weight per hour, or about 1,680 Kcal daily for a 70 kilogram (154 pound) male.[2]

Under normal conditions, the daily caloric requirement recommended by the NRC is 57 Kcal/kg body weight for an active male, or about 4,000 Kcal/day for a 70 kg male.[1] However, under the extremes of exercise, temperature and altitude encountered on expeditions, this daily kilocalorie requirement can be greatly increased.

Exercise may increase expenditure 5 to 10 Kcal/kg/hr. In a cold environment, resting energy expenditure may increase 10 to 40%. The basal metabolic rate increases 10% for each 1,000 meter rise in elevation. Therefore, caloric requirements for high altitude can exceed 6,000 Kcal/day. Daily caloric needs can be calculated based on the formula:

caloric intake = basal metabolic rate +
exercise +
temperature maintenance +
altitude requirements.[3]

EFFECTS OF ALTITUDE ON NUTRITION
Undernutrition

Weight loss at altitude is due to an inadequate energy intake relative to the overall body requirement. This is due to lack of appetite, difficulty in food preparation, reduction in the efficiency of food utilization, poor toleration or absorption of certain diets, gastrointestinal infections, increased body protein breakdown, disturbances in nutrient metabolism, and the effects of increased work load and decreased temperature.[5] In addition, dehydration plays a major role in weight loss and symptoms of acute mountain sickness.

Headache, nausea and vomiting commonly exerienced when ascending into the mountains deaden the appetite. The resulting decreased food intake is the basis of loss of weight upon acute exposure to altitude.[6] In women, the duration of decreased food intake and subsequent weight loss seems to be less than in men under similar conditions.[5]

In general, the period of low intake of nutrients in lowlanders during acute exposure to high altitude is so brief as to present no nutritional problems.[6] Anorexia is maximum during the first three days of exposure, with protein and caloric intakes decreased as much and 30 to 40%, respectively.[7]

The degree of appetite loss may be enhanced when subjects are provided diets of poor palatability.[5] Climbers often go hungry at high altitude rather than eat food which they do not crave. Menus should consist of foods known to be enjoyed by all party members, and special foods to satisfy individual tastes must also be carried.[8] Anorexia, for whatever reason, appears to be the major reason for inadequate caloric intake.[3]

Difficulty or apathy about preparing food at altitude, when complicated by a poor appetite, results in caloric deficits in relation to energy expenditures, leading to weight loss and dehydration.[9]

The higher the altitude, the less oxygen available to metabolize food. Proteins and fats are more complex foods than carbohydrates, and therefore are harder to digest and utilize at altitude. Carbohydrates require 8 to 10% less oxygen for metabolism than do fats or proteins.[4]

Fat and xylose malabsorption occurs in many individuals at high altitude[10] with production of fat in stools. This may explain why climbers appear to perform better on low fat diets at altitude.[7] Intestinal malabsorption might occur secondary to poor blood flow to the intestinal wall, decreased digestive enzyme production, gastrointestinal infections,[7] and/or decreased motility of the small intestine.[6]

Abdominal cramps and diarrhea are frequently encountered at altitude and are often caused by infestation with gastrointestinal bacteria or parasites acquired from unsanitary food and water on the approach march. Such conditions further cause weight loss due to decreased food intake.[11]

The diminished intake of food is unable to provide the level of energy required to sustain activity at high altitude and the deficit has to be made up by breakdown of body tissues. Loss of body weight occurs initially due to loss of stored body fat. More prolonged stays at extreme altitude lead to emaciation with loss of muscle and body nitrogen.[6]

Weight and skin fold determinations used to discover the type and amount of weight loss on a recent Himalayan expedition indicated that weight loss exceeded that explained by decreased body fat alone, implying a negative nitrogen balance. The average body weight loss was 16% with an average body fat loss of 10%. Therefore, weight decrease exceeded that accounted for by decreased body fat alone, suggesting both a negative caloric and a negative nitrogen balance.[3]

At moderate altitudes, loss of body fat is most significant, which accounts for 70% of the weight loss. At higher elevations, loss of fat accounts for only 27% of the weight loss, muscle wasting believed to account for most of the remainder. Protein breakdown seems to occur before fat stores are fully utilized despite the presence of adequate carbohydrates for protein sparing. Therefore, having more body fat available for energy needs at high altitude does not confer an advantage.[7]

Other hypotheses advanced to explain loss of body weight at altitude include a transient abnormality of protein metabolism and disturbances of intermediary metabolism.[6] Many biochemical abnormalities observed can be directly related to lack of eating in acute exposure to altitude rather than a direct effect of decreased oxygen.[12] Possible alterations in protein metabolism cause striking weight loss at extreme altitude.[10] There may be some impairment in protein biosynthesis during the first week of altitude exposure.[12]

Increases in exercise contribute significantly to weight loss at moderate altitude,[7] and with many days of strenuous work and an inadequate caloric intake, glycogen resynthesis in liver and muscle may be reduced.[13] An increased caloric need during acute high altitude exposure may be secondary to the increased cost of cardiac and respiratory work and/or to decreased efficiency of work performance.[12] Simultaneous exposure to cold and low oxygen levels at altitude can cause an increase in basal metabolism.[14]

The result of prolonged stays at altitude result in high altitude cachexia (HAC) which is the physical and mental deterioration observed with exposure to high altitude. The question arises whether HAC is an obligate effect of altitude, or whether it is simply a problem of negative caloric balance.[3] From the evidence given above, undernutrition seems to be the major cause of many problems encountered at high altitude, but other factors must also be involved. Much evidence also points to dehydration as a major cause of weight loss and maladjustment to altitude.

Dehydration

Weight losses not due to calorie restriction are probably the result of underhydration during early altitude exposure.[12] The initial weight loss from dehydration at high altitude reflects a significant drop in total body water, mostly from a decreased plasma volume. The dehydration is due in part to decreased intake and in part due to increased losses resulting from the increased ventilation of cold, dry air[7] and to the diuretic effect of altitude exposure. The latter may be an adaptive response of the body to the hypoxic environment.[12] Climbers may become dehydrated due to the increased pulmonary ventilation induced by elevation and exercise, coupled with the low humidity of the ambient air.[6] Greater respiratory efforts required at high altitudes increase the amount of water required to moisten the inspired air. Furthermore, cold air with a high relative humidity, when warmed to body temperature as it passes from the nose to the lungs, requires more water to provide a relative humidity near 100% while in the lungs. With open mouth breathing, almost all of the moisture in expired air is lost.[8] Water losses through breathing at altitude can run as high as three liters per day.[3] Sweating with exertion adds to body water loss, as does unavailability of water for drinking.[8] Along with sweating, dehydration can account for up to 8% of the total body weight loss.[3]

The need to rehydrate oneself often exceeds the senses, so one does not feel like drinking, even in the face of dehydration.[3] Such dehydration is further aggravated by dulling of the sensation of thirst which accompanies the loss of appetite, nausea, headache and vomiting that occurs with acute mountain sickness. Such dehydration contributes to the depression, impaired judgement and lassitude which further depresses voluntary water intake.[8]

CALORIE AND WATER INTAKE

When planning food for an expedition to high, cold altitudes, allow 5,000 to 6,000 Kcal/person/day.[3]

Himalayan parties have reported that the average caloric intake during approach marches was 4,250 Kcal/day. However, intake fell to 3,100 Kcal/day between 5,000 and 6,700 meters to 1,500 Kcal/day above 7,300 meters.[8][15] This was due to a combination of poor appetite due to high altitude, anorexia and the difficulties of wilderness cooking. The same expeditions calculated energy expenditure from respiratory tests and the results suggested a daily expenditure of up to 3,900 Kcal on hard days, so there appeared to be a considerable energy deficit.[15] Another study indicated the energy expenditure between altitudes of 2,700 and 4,500 meters to be 4,200 Kcal/day as opposed to 3,200 Kcal/day at sea level.[16] On a recent Himalayan trip, climbers between 5,000 and 7,000 meters ate 3,000 to 5,000 Kcal/day. The diet was composed of carbohydrates (55% of calories), fat (35% of calories) and protein (10% of calories).[3]

Analysis of meal composition on expeditions shows a preference for meals higher in carbohydrates while at high altitude and a shift away from fats and protein.[7] On higher carbohydrate, lower fat intake (68% and 20% of calories, respectively) it has been shown that men had considerably better performance in heaviest work and less clinical symptoms at altitude as compared to those on a diet of 48% of calories from carbohydrates and 40% of calories from fat. High carbohydrate meals enhance glucose metabolism at high altitude and increase pulmonary diffusing capacity and work performance.[17] Elevated carbohydrates in the diet enhance altitude tolerance, reduce severity of acute mountain sickness and improve physical performance.[5] Carbohydrates require 8 to 10% less oxygen for metabolism than do fats or proteins.[4]

Recommended Water Intake

At sea level, an average individual requires about 2 liters of fluid per day. At altitude, especially above 4,800 meters, requirements often exceed 4 liters/day.[8] Reports for and recommendations of fluid intakes for high altitude expeditions run from 2 to 5 liters/day between 5,000 and 7,000 meters[3] [15] to 6 to 7 liters/day.[3] Combining fluids with foods increases caloric intake at the same time as rehydration. Cocoa, jello, egg nog, fruit juices and soups are good examples of this type of calorie and fluid combination.[3] Other fluids may be taken as water, tea, coffee, and bouillon.

Caffeine has a diuretic effect and is not recommended in beverages taken at very high altitudes, as the caffeine boost is not worth the resulting dehydration.

To make hydration as simple and available as possible, the use of an insulated 1 liter wide-mouth polyethylene bottle is recommended. It should always be filled with treated water or other beverage and kept handy, especially at night. At night, the bottle can be filled with hot water and used as a hot water bottle in one's sleeping bag, assuring an unfrozen water supply until morning.

SUMMARY

- At high altitude, carbohydrates should provide 60 to 65% of daily caloric intake.
- At high altitude, fats should provide 20 to 25% of daily caloric intake.
- At high altitude, protein should provide 10 to 20% of daily caloric intake.
- Vitamin and mineral supplementation at twice the recommended dosage is suggested on extended trips.
- The basal metabolic rate requires 1 Kcal/kg of body weight/hour or about 1,680 Kcal/day for a 70 kg male (154 pounds).
- In addition to the basal metabolic rate, daily caloric requirements are 57 Kcal/kg of body weight/day or about 4,000 Kcal/day for a 70 kg active male.
- Exercise can increase caloric expenditure 5 to 10 Kcal/kg/hour.

- Cold environments can increase the basal metabolic rate 10 to 40%
- The basal metabolic rate increases 10% for each 1,000 meter rise in elevation.
- Undernutrition and dehydration are the major causes of weight loss at altitude.
- Water losses from respiration at high altitude and cold temperatures can be as high as 3 liters/day.
- Allow 5,000 to 6,000 Kcal/person/day in cold, high altitude situations.
- At high altitude, diets higher in carbohydrates and lower in fat and protein are tolerated better, improve work performance, enhance tolerance to altitude and reduce the severity of acute mountain sickness.
- At high altitude, people show a preference for meals higher in carbohydrates and lower in fat and protein.
- A water intake of 5 to 7 liters/day at high altitude is recommended.

REFERENCES

1. J.D. Kirschmann, *Nutrition Almanac* 4th ed. New York: McGraw-Hill Book Company, 1979: pp. 7-11.
2. E. Peters, *Mountaineering – The Freedom of the Hills* 4th ed. Seattle: The Mountaineers, 1982: pp. 520- 528.
3. E. Hixson, Adirondack Surgical Group, Saranac Lake, New York: Personal communication, 1986.
4. N. Clark, "Expedition Nutrition: Tips for Menu Planning" *Climbing* Aug. 1986: pp. 66-70.
5. J.P. Hannon, G.J. Klain, D.M. Sudman, F.J. Sullivan, "Nutritional Aspects of High-altitude Exposure in Women" *American Journal of Clinical Nutrition* 1976; 29: pp. 604-613.
6. D. Heath and D.R. Williams *Man at High Altitude: The Pathophysiology of Acclimatization and Adaptation.* 2nd ed. New York: Churchill Livingstone, 1981: pp. 209-222.
7. S.J. Boyer and F.D. Blume "Weight Loss and Changes in Body Composition at High Altitude" *Journal of Applied Physiology* 1984; 57: pp. 1580-1585.

8. J.A. Wilkerson, *Medicine for Mountaineering* 2nd ed. Seattle: The Mountaineers, 1975: pp. 149-150.

9. J.S. Milledge, "Arterial Oxygen Desaturation and Intestinal Absorption of Xylose" *British Medical Journal*, 1972; 3: pp. 557-558.

10. J.B. West, "Human Physiology at Extreme Altitudes on Mount Everest" *Science* 1984; 223: pp. 784-788.

11. D. Rennie and R. Wilson "Who Should Not Go High" In: J.R. Sutton, N.L. Jones, and C.S. Houston, eds. *Hypoxia: Man at Altitude* New York: Thieme-Stratton Inc., 1982: pp. 186- 190.

12. C.F. Consolazio, H.L. Johnson, H.J. Krzywicki, and T.A. Daws. "Metabolic Aspects of Acute Altitude Exposure (4,300 m) in Adequately Nourished Humans" *American Journal of Clinical Nutrition* 1972; 25: pp. 23-29.

13. J.R. Sutton, N.L. Jones, L. Griffith, and C.E. Pugh. "Exercise at Altitude" *Annual Review of Physiology* 1983; 45: pp. 427-437.

14. C.S. Nair, M.S. Malhotra, and P.M. Gopinath. "Effect of Altitude and Cold Acclimatization on the Basal Metabolism in Man" *Aerospace Medicine* 1971; 42: p. 1056.

15. L. Griffith and C.E. Pugh. "Mt. Cho Oyu, 1952, and Mt. Everest, 1953" In: J.R. Sutton, N.L. Jones, and C.S. Houston, eds. *Hypoxia: Man at Altitude* New York: Thieme-Stratton Inc., 1982: pp. 108-112.

16. R.M. Rai, M.S. Malhotra, G.P. Dimri, and T. Sampathkumar. "Utilization of Different Quantities of Fat at High Altitude" *American Journal of Clinical Nutrition* 1975; 28: pp. 242-245.

17. R.S. Goodhart and M.E. Shils. *Modern Nutrition in Health and Disease* 6th ed. Philadelphia: Lea and Febiger, 1980: p. 838.

Chapter 3

Food and Menu Planning

". . . alpine cuisine is not an exact science, but a true art form."

MOUNTAINEERING: THE FREEDOM OF THE HILLS

*P*LANNING THE NUTRITIONAL needs for a high mountain expedition must be based on a firm understanding of basic nutrition and the effects of altitude on food utilization. These points were discussed in the previous chapter. Other requirements for successful planning naturally involve individual preferences, the number of people in the group and the duration of the trip.

DIETARY QUESTIONNAIRE

In order to provide the best possible nutrition to members of the group, it is advisable to obtain personalized dietary information. This can be accomplished in the form of a dietary questionnaire that will alert you to special individual dietary needs or restrictions. This information will be invaluable in further food planning. An example of a dietary questionnaire can be found at the end of this chapter.

DETERMINING QUANTITIES OF FOOD STOCKS

If the expedition is to progress in "pyramid" fashion, the majority of food supplies will first be moved to the basecamp area, and progressively smaller deposits will be left at successive camps until the furthest camp is supplied only with enough material to support activity from that point (with extra for emergency use). During the process of moving supplies to advanced camps, some of the food is used by persons ferrying the loads and this must be taken into account when planning a food inventory for each camp.

Man-days

In determining the basic amount of food to take, a figure expressed in "man-days" is very helpful. To determine this figure, the number of persons on the trip is multiplied by the length of the trip in days. For example:

$$10 \text{ men} \times 90 \text{ days} = 900 \text{ man-days}$$

This means there will be 900 breakfasts, 900 lunches and 900 dinners. This figure represents the amount of food necessary to feed each man daily for the duration of the trip. Usually, extra food is taken to serve in emergencies or to replace food lost or damaged *en route* or to cover for travel delays.

Some expedition food lists are based on weight, with 1½ to 2 pounds of food allotted per person per day (dehydrated foods). However, because moisture and weight of foods vary greatly, planning food lists by weight can be misleading, especially if high moisture canned or packaged foods (in a pliable foil pouch) are used. Also, a certain amount of one type of food may be very low in calories or protein, whereas the same amount of another food may be very high. Based on such ambiguities, I prefer to use man-days and total calories as a basis for planning the menu and food list. With proper food item choices and if total calories are met, protein needs are also provided.

Daily Caloric Needs

After computing the number of man-days, this figure can be use along with daily caloric needs per man to determine total daily caloric needs. The climate, season, elevation and work load must be estimated. Referring to caloric needs stated in Chapter 2, an example of 10 men for 90 days in winter conditions at high altitude with heavy work could mean 900 man-days, each consisting of 4,000 calories (Kcal). This figure will give a basis from which to determine the total amount of food to procure.

Local Food Availability

Before planning a shopping list, one may want to consider availability of local foods which can be purchased in the country of destination. One must take into consideration the season (is it harvest time?), droughts causing crop failure, local famine, and size of cities or villages along the way. If these factors are known, one can determine what foods may be available. Buying local foods can reduce food costs and decrease the effort and cost of packing and shipping food from the point of origin of the expediton. Care must be taken to assure that the food locally purchased will be safe to eat, however. Grains, vegetables, and fruits, if properly washed and prepared, are usually safe, whereas dairy and egg products or meats can transmit diseases to man.

Type of Food

The type of expedition, fuel availability, storage capabilities, and manner and ease with which food can be prepared determine the type of foods to buy. An expedition to Antarctica which requires frequent moving of camps further inland, for example, will require lightweight, easy to prepare foods which do not consume large quantities of fuel during preparation and can be quickly and easily prepared in the extreme polar environment. On the other hand, an expedition staying in a semipermanent camp in a temperate environment closer to civilization can afford the luxury of meals prepared from less highly processed foods, often with frequent additions of available fresh fruits and vegetables. The goal is to produce palatable, nutritious meals, while at the same time conserving fuel, making food preparation and cleanup as easy as possible and using food supplies prudently.

Meal Planning

Once one has a firm idea of the total man-days of food and its caloric density, and takes into consideration additions of local foods and the type of food that best suits one's particular needs, meals can be planned more accurately according to the following steps:

1. For example, breakfast is usually a full meal prepared and eaten in camp, and should constitute about ⅕ of the total daily caloric intake. Start by listing all of the varieties of breakfast foods you would like to have on the trip. For example:

powdered eggs	canned ham, bacon, or hash
pancake mix	hot and cold cereals
pastries	freeze-dried sausage patties

At this point, you will have to perform some calculations in order to determine quantities of breakfast items to purchase. In most instances, even based on man-days and caloric value, a broad range results.

Values for servings per package and calories per serving are printed on the package and these figures are used for calculation guidelines. Also, books listing caloric density of many common foods are available and can be quite useful.

2. The following calculation will help illustrate the method for determining amounts of food for breakfast for a party of 10 men for 90 days:

10 men × 90 days = 900 man-days

900 man-days × 4,000 Kcal/man/day = 3,600,000 Kcal for 10 men for 90 days

If breakfast provides ⅕ of total daily calories, then 3,600,000 ÷ 5 = 720,000 Kcal to be provided by breakfast

3. Next, determine the Kcal/serving for each item from the package or other source:

eggs	150 Kcal/serving
pancake mix	300 Kcal/serving
freeze-dried sausage	300 Kcal/serving
ham, bacon, or hash	200 Kcal/serving
hot and cold cereal	150 Kcal/serving
pastries	200 Kcal/serving

Obviously, some items have much lower caloric density than others, requiring twice as much to provide the same number of calories. Therefore, low calorie foods should be combined in a meal with higher calorie foods to help provide the necessary energy.

4. At this point, it must be realized that a breakfast consisting of 800 Kcal (4,000 Kcal/day ÷ 5) must be designed for each man for each day, and it may be difficult for that much food to be consumed. However, it must be provided and the people encouraged to eat. That is where palatability is important!

5. Now, estimate the number of calories to be provided by each different item to result in a total of 720,000 Kcal:

eggs	120,000 Kcal
pancakes	110,000 Kcal
sausage	125,000 Kcal
ham, bacon, or hash	125,000 Kcal
hot and cold cereal	120,000 Kcal
pastries	120,000 Kcal
Total:	720,000 Kcal

Most meals will consist of two or three of the above items (i.e. eggs, bacon, and a pastry).

6. Next, divide the calories to be provided by a food type by its calories/serving to determine the total number of servings needed:

eggs	120,000 ÷ 150	= 800 servings
pancakes	110,000 ÷ 300	= 367 servings
sausage	125,000 ÷ 300	= 417 servings
ham, bacon, or hash	125,000 ÷ 200	= 625 servings
hot and cold cereal	120,000 ÷ 150	= 800 servings
pastries	120,000 ÷ 200	= 600 servings

From this, it seems that there is an over abundance of breakfast item servings. It is important to remember that the figure of calories per serving obtained from the package or other source is based on a serving size for an average person on an average day at an average altitude, and is too little for hard, high-altitude work in cold temperatures.

Therefore, based on the above calculations, 800 servings of eggs should be taken and the daily serving size increased proportionately to provide adequate calories.

Calculations up to this point must be done before procuring food items, so an estimate of total amounts of each food to be obtained can be made. From this point, menus can be planned on a daily basis in camp, if desired.

DAILY MENU PLANNING

From the previous information, daily menus can be made which will provide adequate calories. Appendix VIII lists sample menus for one week, based on the recipes in Chapters 9 and 10.

Breakfast

Some juggling must be done here, and servings increased by trial and error to obtain the total calories necessary:

10 men × 1 breakfast = 10 men × 800 Kcal = 8,000 Kcal
eggs   200 Kcal × 10 = 2,000 Kcal (1¼ normal serv-
            ings/man)
bacon   400 Kcal × 10 = 4,000 Kcal (2 normal servings/
            man)
pastry   200 Kcal × 10 = 2,000 Kcal (1 normal serving/
            man)

TOTAL: 8,000 Kcal

In this way, serving sizes can be increased to provide necessary calories for each man for each day. The same process is repeated for lunch, dinner, snacks, and drinks.

Lunch, Snacks, and Desserts

These items should equal about ⅔ of daily calories, and this figure is used to calculate quantities needed. In many instances, lunch is a lighter meal made up of "trail foods" and snacks which can be taken along on the trail or route while work is being completed. Examples of such foods are:

meat spreads	peanut butter
jerky	granola
crackers	candy bars
cheese spreads	fruit (fresh, dried, leather)

These are divided up just as the breakfast items were to obtain the number of servings of each to take along to provide ⅔ of daily caloric needs.

Dinner

Dinner should provide ⅕ of total daily caloric intake and items can be chosen and servings calculated as above.

Drinks

Drinks, including breakfast drinks, fruit punches, cider, nog, cocoa, and soups should constitute the last ⅕ of daily caloric intake and can be consumed throughout the day to ensure hydration and provide the remainder of the day's calories.

Approach Food

In addition to the above foods and quantities, it may be desirable to pack other parcels of food to be eaten while journeying to the last outpost of civilization, when the main cache of expedition food starts to be consumed. This "approach" food can be used to vary or increase food intake, to augment poor local cuisine and to provide safe snack foods on airplane layovers, travel delay days and similar situations.

Miscellaneous

In addition to major food supplies, condiments, spices and other miscellaneous food items which do not necessarily provide significant calories will have to be planned and procured to help complete the food item list and to add variety and flavor to basic food items.

DIETARY QUESTIONNAIRE

1. Name _____

2. Weight _____ Height _____ Age _____ Sex _____

3. Check your current physical status:
   Excellent in strength and endurance ___ good ___ fair ___ poor ___

4. Describe your daily excerise or other physical conditioning program:

5. Do you take daily vitamin supplementation? yes ___ no ___

6. Do you have any food allergies? yes ___ no ___
   If so, describe problem foods and type of reaction:

7. Do you have any religious dietary restrictions? yes ___ no ___
   If so, describe:

8. Are you a vegetarian? yes ___ no ___
   Do you eat eggs? yes ___ no ___
   Do you eat dairy products? yes ___ no ___

9. If you have any strong dislikes for certain foods, please list:

10. What are your favorite foods and sweets?

11. What is your approximate caloric intake on an average day?

12. Comments:

Chapter 4

Food Procurement and Shipping

*A*FTER THE LIST OF FOODS to buy has been made, based on the points mentioned in Chapter 3, it is time to procure the food, repackage some items, and box them for shipment.

SPONSORSHIP AND DONATIONS

Because of the great expense of most major expeditions, funds are usually short and economy must be emphasized. Expeditions to remote locations, particularly those with exotic objectives, can often barter some of their glamour for food and equipment at reduced prices – even free.

Many foods can be obtained as donations from food product companies; it is a form of advertisement for their products. The companies usually only require photographs of their products being used during the expedition or a written endorsement of their product. Often, special foods can be obtained if they seem particularly suited to your expedition (i.e. vegetarian, special packaging).

The company or a sales representative is contacted via letter or telephone and your purpose stated. (Use expedition letterhead stationery to increase credibility.) Depending on the financial status of the company and the value of such advertising, they may or may not sponsor your trip with food gifts. Some will give only limited quantities, whereas others are quite generous. In general, most are willing to provide their products to major expeditions. In return, several hours of photographing products in use on the expedition or composing endorsements fulfills your obligation, but this task should be promptly and conscientiously performed. Do not request, use and endorse two competitive products from two different companies.

Such donations should be sought as early as possible, as it can take several months for the items to be shipped, especially if some are on backorder at the company.

PURCHASING FOOD

After food donation commitments have been made and those items marked off the shopping list, the remainder must be purchased. Again, economy is the watchword.

The local grocery chain or grocery distributor is an excellent place to start buying products, usually at a more reasonable price than specialty backpacking foods. Another advantage to buying from your grocer or his distributor is familiarity with the product and access to your favorite brands.

Buying from product companies or distributors and buying in bulk enables substantial savings over retail dealers. Prices may vary between or among dealers and prices are subject to change. New products are constantly being introduced by companies. Sometimes they offer close-out prices on items.

Shop around for the best deals, again, a process that should begin months in advance of your departure date. Since the foods you will use on the expedition are the types that need no refrigeration and have very long shelf lives, buying early is to your advantage, especially to ensure that products ordered by mail will arrive in time for repacking if necessary, boxing and shipping.

At this point, decisions must be made whether foods should be bought in sizes packaged for individual use, small groups (2 to 4 people) or bulk. As a rule, bulk supplies and minimally processed foods are less expensive, but likewise less convenient because they require division and repackaging into smaller portions and usually require more preparation while cooking. On the other hand, although individual or 2 to 4 person serving packages are convenient, all the packaging may be heavy and poses a disposal problem in camp. In addition, heavily processed foods may not be as palatable or nutritious as less highly processed foods. In general, a balance between the two extremes is made. Certain items (cocoa, hot nog, and other hot drink mixes) are most easy to use from individual packets and allow each member of the expedition to make his own choice, whereas spaghetti dinner for 10 is much more palatable and less expensive to prepare from bulk supplies than from many, expensive, individual pouches of freeze dried products, often resulting in inferior tasting "mush".

Jam, honey, peanut butter, coffee, meats, brown bread, cooking oil, some condiments, spices, dry milk, ketchup, condensed and sweetened condensed milk, dehydrated potatoes, biscuits, and crackers should be bought in canned form. It is heavy, but also most durable. If canned forms are only available in larger sizes, they can be broken up into smaller portions after arrival in basecamp. Try to obtain plastic lids to use on opened cans to protect their contents.

Although plastic, foil, paper, and cardboard packaging is light and not bulky, they are easily torn during transport, or cardboard "melts" in the rain. Contents spill, damaging other foods and rendering the product susceptible to invasion by rodents and insects. Such packaging does have the advantage of being burnable, whereas cans must be properly disposed. However, empty, washed #10 cans have many convenient uses around camp (utensil holders, toilet paper holder at the latrine, storage for teabags, tent garbage cans).

Individual use packages of mayonnaise, mustard, ketchup, soysauce and relish can be purchased from restaurant suppliers and are especially good for items perishable if opened in large quantities. However, if taken from very low to very high altitudes, they can burst and spill their contents. The packages must be protected from trauma during travel to prevent damage.

The costs of foods will naturally vary from retailer to retailer, and often close-outs or other sales can by found to help cut costs. As a general rule, the more highly processed and convenient the food, and the smaller the packaged amount, the higher the price.

Freeze dried foods of any type are more expensive than their dehydrated or dried counterparts. Foods purchased in specialty "backpacking" stores are usually much more expensive than foods purchased through a retail grocer, which in turn is more expensive than a wholesale grocery distributor.

The type of packaging can greatly affect price. Individually packaged foods are much more expensive than the same food in bulk amounts. Also, foods packaged so as to require no refrigeration, such as retort pouches, are quite expensive. Cans can be economical, but are heavy and shipping costs can be very costly.

REPACKAGING AND BOXING FOR SHIPMENT

After donated foods have arrived and other food supplies have been purchased, decisions about repackaging must be made and the foods packed for shipment.

When repacking bulk items, decide if the product is to be packaged in individual serving sizes, 2, 4, 8 or more person pouches, or merely divided so that some gets to each camp. In any case, make sure the product is durably repackaged, labeled, dated, its destination marked on the package, and instructions for preparation included. The latter can be xeroxed from the original package or instructions and placed in the repackaged items.

Placing items in cartons at home for shipment takes a great deal of forethought and planning. Do not pack all of one type of food in one carton; if that box is lost or damaged, all of that item is gone. Boxing food and supplies for shipment can be accomplished in several ways. 1) Box for the camp of destination. Such a box contains items destined to reach a certain camp, so repacking is unnecessary. 2) Box according to meal. Such a box contains items used mainly for preparing breakfasts (or lunch or dinner). 3) Box per each day. Items for each meal during the day are packed in one box, requiring only one box to be opened to find everything necessary for one day (or several days, depending on box size and group size).

While packing foods, consider packing contents of each meal in a sack of its own. This method is especially helpful for smaller, shorter trips with well-defined numbers of people in camp. For larger expeditions with many people in different camps for undefined amounts of time, it is easier to just break down bulk foods into smaller, more usable sizes for division among camps, and boxing of foods so that not all of the same food is in the same box, so that the boxes can be distributed to different camps without first being broken up. In either event, most of the food should be in its most convenient form before leaving home to minimize weight, waste, and rehandling in camp. This also includes repackaged foods being clearly and indelibly marked, preparation instructions included in bulk foods that have been divided and placed in containers that will not leak, puncture, spill, shatter, seep, stain, contaminate, or blow away. Likewise, the packaged food must be protected from dirt, water, tainting from soaps, cleaners, oils, and strong foods. Paper labels on cans should be either taped in place or the label removed and the can labeled directly on the metal with a felt-tipped pen.

PACKING LIST

Whatever method of boxing is used based on your needs or desires, it is imperative to make a packing list as you go, noting quantities, weights, and types of items in each box. The list should be as thorough as possible and should list the individual weight of each box. The list should be xeroxed so several copies exist in case of loss or destruction of the original. The list can also state the destination of each box.

SHIPMENT

The type of shipping employed throughout the trip must be considered so shipping weights and regulations can be met as boxes are packed. Means of shipping your boxed goods include air freight, ocean-going "slow boat," and overland or surface freight.

Any cartons shipped by air freight must be done in accordance with the carrier service to be used. Because all regulations are not uniform, check with the airlines you are using to determine dimensions, weights, and carton board test (box strength) required. Air freight is quick and can usually accompany expedition members on the same flights. It also allows for packing to go on right up to the last minute and therefore is very convenient, but it is very expensive.

Freighting supplies by ship is much less expensive than by air, but requires that the shipment be made well in advance of the departure of expedition members. Therefore, all planning, procurement, and boxing must be done very early. Arrangements must be made for the unloading and storage of the shipment in the country of destination until the expedition arrives. As with air freight, check with the shipping authority for shipment requirements.

Depending on the country of destination, surface shipping can mean anything from a taxi to a yak. While planning travel in the country of destination, avoid repacking by planning your boxing according to the type of surface shipment to be used. Mainly to be considered are weight, box dimensions, and box durability. The following are average weights carried by various beasts of burden:

Man: 40 to 60 pounds
Yak: 55 pounds per side = 110 pounds
Camel: up to 330 pounds, depending on terrain, temperature and altitude. The usual regulation is 175 pounds.
Horse or mule 50 pounds per side = 100 pounds
Donkey or burro: 30 pounds per side = 60 pounds
Llama: 45 pounds

SOURCES OF CARTON MATERIALS

Check the local yellow pages in the telephone directory under "Boxes" to find area container manufacturers. They can help determine needs for 1) size dimensions, 2) board test (a product of papers and flute heights which determine strength of the box), 3) Assemblage "Knocked down flat" with glue holding the main seam; these boxes assemble with flaps top and bottom that close without a gap. Apple carton type boxes are also available, with two components, a bottom portion over which fits a complete top. 4) Weatherproofing or weather-resistance capabilities (can be waxed inside and/or outside, or wet strength paper with weatherproof starch adhesive to hold the box together.) 5) Cardboard barrels with ring clamp closure and metal lids. 6) Plastic barrels with ring clamp or screw top closures.

In addition to the containers mentioned above, sources of used cartons should be investigated, as this may result in great saving in cost. All boxes should be sealed with wide strapping tape and carefully labeled in accordance with the packing list and the title and address of the expedition.

FOOD CHART

The following list of food products is only partial and is designed to give examples of many currently available products well suited for expeditions requiring light-weight or convenient foods which require no refrigeration. The chart is meant to be an aid and guide to inform you of the many specialty products and packaging forms available. A list of addresses of companies represented in the chart can be found in Appendix VI. In addition, the chart contains many bulk forms of products.

Many popular backpacking, camping and expedition foods are not listed (canned tuna, ramen, oatmeal, coffee and candy bars) as these are readily available products that can be easily obtained in all areas of the United States and, if necessary, pricing and product information can be obtained from your local grocer.

DESCRIPTION	PACKAGING	PREPARATION	REFERENCE
	Baking Mixes		
Buckwheat, whole wheat and whole wheat plus soy pancake mixes	32 oz paper bag	Mix with egg and milk and cook	Stone Buhr
Blueberry or buttermilk pancake mixes	2 or 4 person pouch	Add water and cook	Richmoor
Cakes, brownies, pancake mix, cookies, cheesecakes, pie and pizza crust, quiche custard mix, muffins, biscuits, yeast dough mixes	Various sizes and canned or poly bag packaging (5 lb bag or #10 can)	Add water and bake	Bernard
Biscuits, cornbread, brownie, gingerbread, pancake and French toast mixes	4 person pouch	Add water and bake	Stow-a-way
White or whole wheat bread mix, brownie, wheat or corn muffin, pancake, cookie, biscuit, sourdough bread, English muffin mixes	18 oz bags	Add water and bake	Yurika
Buckwheat or blueberry pancake mixes	3 or 6 person pouch	Add water and cook	Alpine Aire
Pancake, muffin, bread, biscuit, cornbread, carob cake mixes	9 to 32 oz poly packages; some available in 25 lb bags	Require mixing, some with addition of egg, and baking	Arrowhead Mills

DESCRIPTION	PACKAGING	PREPARATION	REFERENCE
Coffee cake, buttermilk pancakes, French toast, applesauce cake mix	2 or 4 person pouch	Mix with water and bake	Dri-Lite
Bread and roll mix, buttermilk pancake mix	#10 cans	Mix with water and bake	Survival Supply Ready Reserve
Variety pancake mixes	2 or 4 person pouch	Mix with water and bake	Survival Supply Wee Pak
Beans, Seeds, and Nuts			
Adzuki, black, blackeye, chickpeas, Great Northern, mung, kidney, lima, lentils, navy, pinto, soy, split peas, alfalfa seeds, flax seed, sesame, sunflower, peanuts, amaranth, almonds, pecans	12 to 24 oz cello bags (also 25 to 50 lb bags)	Beans need long cooking or sprouting, seeds and nuts good to eat as is or use in cooking	Arrowhead Mills
Navy, pinto, and chili beans, wheat, Alaskan peas, lentils, triticale	#10 cans or #2½ cans	See above	Perma Pak
"Instantized" lima, blackeye peas, black, Great Northern, navy, pinto, kidney and red beans	25 or 50 lb box	Shorter cooking time than regular beans and no presoaking needed	Bernard
Lima, garbanzo, mung, pinto, kidney, soy, lentils, split peas, white beans	#10 cans; some available in 33-36 lb bucket	Lengthy cooking time; good for sprouting	Stow-a-way
Flaxseed, mung, poppyseed, soybeans and sesame	7 oz to 2 lb bags	Good for sprouting and for use in cooking	Pavo

DESCRIPTION	PACKAGING	PREPARATION	REFERENCE
Brazil nuts	10 oz packages	Eat as is or use for cooking	Timber Crest
Freeze dried pinto beans, lentils, small white beans	2 person pouch or 3 to 4 lb bags	Add water and cook a very short time	Alpine Aire
Flaxseed, sesame, sunflower seeds	21 to 26 oz poly bags	Use in cooking	Stone Buhr
Alaskan peas, lentils, triticale	#2½ cans	Good for sprouting and for use in cooking	Survival Supply Ready Reserve
Navy, pinto, chili bean	#10 cans	Lengthy cooking time	Survival Supply Ready Reserve
Cereals, Flakes, and Granolas			
Rolled oats, cracked wheat, fruit and nut cereal	#10 cans	Add water and cook a short time	Stow-a-way
Bran flakes, oat cereal, rolled oats, whole wheat cereal, wheat germ, buckwheat and oat groats, toasted soy grits	½ to 3 lb pkgs; some available in 25 or 50 lb pkgs	Some require short cooking times; others can be eaten with milk or without cooking	Pavo
Ten-grain cereal	2 lb pkg	Add hot water	Yurika
Fruit mush	2 person or 7 person bulk	Add water and cook a short time	Alpine Aire
Oatmeal with fruit, granola fruit cereal	2 or 4 person pouch	Add milk or hot water	Dri-Lite
Bran flakes, wheat germ, cracked wheat, oats, bulgur, rye flakes, fruit and nut hot cereal	10 to 31 oz boxes or bags	Add water and cook a short time	Stone Buhr

DESCRIPTION	PACKAGING	PREPARATION	REFERENCE
Bulgur, corn, cracked wheat, oat, wheat, bran, 7-grain, barley, rye, triticale flakes, soybean flakes, granola, wheat germ, bear mush	6 to 32 oz poly bags; also in 25 or 50 lb bags	Require moderate to long cooking times. Also good in baking, and granolas can be eaten as is	Arrowhead Mills
Rolled oats, cracked wheat	#2½ and #10 cans	Short cooking time	Perma Pak
Blueberry granola with milk	#10 can or 2 person pouch	Add hot or cold water	Mountain House
Oatmeal or whole wheat cereal with milk and sugar	4 person pouch	Add hot water	Stow-a-way
Granola	#10 cans	Ready to eat or add hot water	Survival Supply Ready Reserve
Granola with blueberries and milk	2 or 4 person pouch	Ready to eat or add hot or cold water	Survival Supply Wee Pak
Cheese and Cheese Sauces			
American or Cheddar cheese powder mix	4 person pouch or #10 can	Sprinkle over food or mix with hot water for sauce	Stow-a-way
Cheddar cheese powder mix	4 oz pouch	Mix with water for sauce or sprinkle over food	Richmoor
Wisconsin cheese powder mix	20 oz bags	Mix with water for sauce or sprinkle over food	Pavo
Cheddar cheese powder mix	3 to 4 oz bags or by the pound	Mix with water for sauce or sprinkle over food	Alpine Aire

DESCRIPTION	PACKAGING	PREPARATION	REFERENCE
Cottage cheese, freeze dried	#10 cans or 2 person pouch	Soak in cold water	Mountain House
Cheddar cheese spread	5.8 lb can	Ready to eat	Mountain House
Cheddar cheese and Nacho cheese sauce bases	#10 can or 18 oz poly bag; 16½ oz can, respectively	Mix with water	Bernard
Cheddar cheese spread	4 person pouch	Ready to spread	Dri-Lite
Cheese blend spread	#2½ can	Ready to spread	Perma Pak
Quiche custard mix	#10 can	Add water and bake in pastry shell	Bernard
Cheese blend	#2½ or #10 cans	Ready to spread	Survival Supply Ready Reserve

Crackers and Bread

DESCRIPTION	PACKAGING	PREPARATION	REFERENCE
Yukon biscuits	#2½ cans	Ready to eat	Perma Pak
Crackers	#10 can	Ready to eat	Mountain House
Pilot biscuits	9.6 oz bag	Ready to eat	Richmoor
Sliced pumpernickel	1 lb can	Ready to eat	Alpine Aire
Pilot biscuits	4 2-biscuit pkg	Ready to eat	Dry-Lite
Brown bread with raisins	1 lb can	Ready to eat	B & M Company
Yukon biscuits	#2½ can	Ready to eat	Survival Supply Ready Reserve

DESCRIPTION	PACKAGING	PREPARATION	REFERENCE
Pilot biscuits	20 per pkg	Ready to eat	Survival Supply Wee Pak
Dairy and Margarines			
Whole dry milk	2 or 4 person pouch	Add cold water	Survival Supply Wee Pak
Milk, non-fat dry	#2½ and #10 cans	Add cold water	Perma Pak
Milk, non-fat dry	#10 can	Add cold water	Mountain House
Milk, non-fat dry	1, 3, and 25 lb bags	Add cold water	Pavo
Milkman[R] low-fat dry milk	1 qt pkgs	Add cold water	Familiar Foods
Milk, non-fat dry or whole dry	#2½ or #10 cans	Add cold water	Survival Supply Ready Reserve
Whole or non-fat dry milk	4 person pouch	Add cold water	Stow-a-way
Milk, whole dry	4 person pouch	Add cold water	Dri-Lite
Margarine powder	#2½ and #10 cans	Add oil or water or use in baking (do not use for frying)	Perma Pak
Real butter	1 lb can	Ready to use	Darigold
Shortening powder mix and margarine powder mix	#10 can	Add oil or water or use in baking (do not use for frying)	Stow-a-way
Butter powder mix	3 to 4 oz pouch or by the pound	Mix with water	Alpine Aire

DESCRIPTION	PACKAGING	PREPARATION	REFERENCE
Margarine and shortening powder mix	2¾ lb or 12¾ lb cans, respectively	Mix with water	Perma Pak
Margarine spread	4 person pouch	Ready to spread	Dri-Lite
Canned margarine	1¼ lb can	Ready to spread	Stow-a-way
Butter flavored shortening	3½ oz pkg		Stow-a-way
Butter powder	#10 can	Mix with water (do not use for frying)	Stow-a-way
Margarine product, butter product	#2½ or #10 cans	Ready to spread	Survival Supply Ready Reserve

Desserts

DESCRIPTION	PACKAGING	PREPARATION	REFERENCE
Puddings – chocolate, banana, black walnut, coconut, vanilla, raspberry, lemon, butterscotch, tapioca, custard, Viennese creme, flan, mousse, meringue, bread pudding, Bavarian creme	#10 cans or 1 to 2 lb poly bags	Some need milk and cooking; some need water and cooking; some need water only and no cooking	Bernard
Variety flavor gelatins	#10 cans or 12 oz to 4½ lb bags	Add boiling water and set	Bernard
Cheese cake, cobblers, vanilla, chocolate or rice pudding, fruit delight, mousse	2 to 4 person pouch	Add cold water or boiling water and soak or set	Dri-Lite
Chocolate mousse, cheese cake, coconut cream pie, whipped topping	6 person pkg	Add melted butter to crust, add milk to pudding and topping	Jello Brands, General Foods

DESCRIPTION	PACKAGING	PREPARATION	REFERENCE
Freeze dried cobbler, Brown Betty, applesauce, cheese cake, chocolate, vanilla or banana pudding, fruit cocktail, apple compote	2 or 4 person pouch	Add cold or boiling water and soak	Richmoor
Sierra coffee cake	4 person pouch	Add cold water and bake	Richmoor
Chocolate, vanilla or butterscotch pudding, fruit smash, orange, raspberry or strawberry gelatin	4 person pouch or #10 can	Add boiling or cold water and soak or set at room temperature	Stow-a-way
Chocolate or strawberry pudding-mousse dessert	3.2 oz pouch	Add milk and set	Yurika
Brownies, cookies, fruit and nut cakes	3.2 oz pouch	Ready to eat	Survival Supply MRE's
Apple Brown Betty, cobblers, cheese cake, puddings, custards, mousse, shortcake, lemon pie	2 or 4 person pouch	Add water and soak	Survival Supply Wee Pak
Applesauce, apple-almond crisp	2 person pouch	Add water	Alpine Aire
Chocolate, butterscotch and banana pudding	#10 can	Add water and set	Mountain House
Neopolitan ice cream	2 person pouch	Add cold water	Dri-Lite
Orange gelatin	#10 can	Add cold water and set	Perma Pak

DESCRIPTION	PACKAGING	PREPARATION	REFERENCE
	Dinner Entrees		
Smoked salmon, beef stew, chicken cacciatore, Alaskan whitefish, shrimp Creole (each with rice in a separate package)	4 to 7 oz retort	Place pouch in boiling water and heat 5 minutes	Chef-to-go
Sausage and gravy, pasta and beef in tomato sauce, beans and franks, chili, sloppy joe, beef stew, Salisbury steak, roast pork and gravy, turkey and gravy, beef stroganoff, Chinese vegetable, vegetable stew, creamed beef, corned beef hash, chicken a la king, chicken stew (rice and pasta in 4.2 oz pouch)	7 oz retort	Place pouch in boiling water and heat 5 minutes	Smoky Canyon
Salisbury steak, chili and tamales, beef stew, cannelloni, meatballs, cacciatore, sweet and sour pork, menni-cotti, chili, chicken a la king, stroganoff, beef burgundy, cabbage rolls, lasagna, Swiss steak, clam chowder, shrimp Creole, trout almondine (rice and pasta in pouches)	7 to 10 oz retort	Place pouch in boiling water and heat 5 minutes	Yurika
Frankfurters, beef stew, ham slices, spiced beef, chicken a la king, turkey and gravy, barbecue beef slices, barbecue meatballs	4 to 8 oz retort	Place pouch in boiling water and heat 5 minutes	Survival Supply MRE's

DESCRIPTION	PACKAGING	PREPARATION	REFERENCE
Variety of freeze dried dinners	2 to 4 person pouches; Mountain House also has some entrees available in #10 cans	Some require mixing with water and short cooking time. Others only require soaking in hot water. Pre-soaking can speed cooking time.	Richmoor-Natural High, Dri-Lite, Mountain House, Stow-a-way, Alpine Aire, Survival Supply-Wee Pak
Dehydrated (low moisture) dinners in several varieties	4 to 8 person serving cans	Moderate cooking time after addition of water. Pre-soaking can speed cooking.	Perma Pak
Dehydrated	#2½ cans or 3 to 4 person pouches	See above	Survival Supply Ready Reserve
Drink Mixes			
Orange breakfast drink, lemon-lime, cherry, boysenberry, tropical fruit, raspberry	4 person pouch	Add cold water	Dri-Lite
Apple or orange breakfast drink	#10 cans (apple also in #2½ can)	Add cold water	Perma Pak
Cocoa mix, milk shake mix, egg nog	#10 cans, 16 to 32 oz cans, or 32 to 40 oz poly bags	Add hot water to cocoa mix; add milk to nog and shake mixes.	Bernard

DESCRIPTION	PACKAGING	PREPARATION	REFERENCE
Orange juice mix, grapefruit juice, a variety of naturally sweetened fruit drinks	#10 cans or 24 to 36 oz poly bags. Some mixes are available in single serving packages.	Add cold water	Bernard
Hot cider, hot egg nog mix	Individual pkts	Add hot water	Today Food Products
Hot cider, hot egg nog, cocoa, cappuccino	Individual pkts	Add hot water	Red Wagon
Orange or lemon drink mix	#10 cans	Add cold water	Mountain House
Gatorade, fruit punch, orange drink, grape drink, lemonade, grapefruit, tomato, and pineapple juice mix	4 person pouch	Add cold water	Survival Supply Wee Pak
Cocoa, egg nog, hot cider mix	2 person pouch	Add hot water	Survival Supply Wee Pak
Gatorade® in orange or lemon-lime	1 qt or 1 gallon pkgs	Add cold water	Stokely-VanCamp
Lemon, orange, and fruit punch	4 person pouch	Add cold water	Richmoor
Lemon-lime flavored Vitamin C supplement	1 person tablet	Add to cold water	Alpine Aire
Nutri-whey plain or cocoa supplemental drink mix	2 qt pkgs	Add cold or hot water; may add cold milk	Yurika
Instant coffee	Individual pkts	Add hot water	Mountain House

DESCRIPTION	PACKAGING	PREPARATION	REFERENCE
Orange juice, grapefruit juice, orange, grape, tomato, lemonade, chocolate and strawberry milk shake, cocoa, coffee, ERG in regular, fruit punch and lemonade flavor	1 qt or 1 gallon pkg. (Cocoa in #10 cans, coffee in individual pkts)	Add cold or hot water	Stow-a-way
Cocoa	4 person pouch	Add hot water	Dri-Lite
Cocoa, apple or orange breakfast drink	#2½ or #10 cans	Add hot or cold water	Survival Supply Ready Reserve
Eggs			
Cheese or Denver omelette, scrambled eggs with or without bacon	2 or 4 person pouch	Mix with water and cook	Dri-Lite
Egg mix	#2½ or #10 cans	Mix with water and cook	Perma Pak
Cheese omelette, precooked eggs with bacon, eggs with butter	3½ oz bags or #10 cans	Precooked eggs only need to be soaked in hot water. Others are mixed with water and cooked.	Mountain House
Scrambled egg with or without bacon, Western omelette	#10 cans	Add water and cook	Bernard
Scrambled egg with or without bacon, Western omelette	2 or 4 person pouch	Add water and cook	Richmoor

DESCRIPTION	PACKAGING	PREPARATION	REFERENCE
Freeze dried eggs – cooked and uncooked, variety omelettes, eggs with bacon or with bacon and potatoes	2 or 4 person pouch	Add water and cook	Survival Supply Wee Pak
Scrambled eggs with or without bacon, Western omelette	4 person pouch	Add water and cook	Stow-a-way
Scrambling eggs, egg whites, whole eggs	#10 cans	Mix with water and cook	Stow-a-way
Scrambling eggs, omelette mix plain or with cheddar cheese	3 or 4 person pouch (plain eggs also in bulk)	Mix with water and cook	Alpine-Aire
Whole eggs, scrambled egg mix	#2½ or #10 cans or 3 person pouch	Mix with water and cook	Survival Supply Ready Reserve
Flours and Meals			
Barley, brown rice, buckwheat, cornmeal, oat, rye, soy, white, triticale, whole wheat, millet, graham, gluten, amaranth, artichoke, and carob powder	1 oz to 5 lb cello pkgs; also 25 to 50 lb bags	Good for use in baking	Arrowhead Mills
White, whole wheat, cornmeal	#10 cans	Good for use in baking	Perma Pak
White, whole wheat, cornmeal	#10 cans	Good for use in baking	Stow-a-way
Cornmeal, alfalfa leaf, rye, buckwheat, potato, white, whole wheat	8 oz to 8 lb pkgs; some also in 25 and 50 lb bags	Good for use in baking	Pavo

DESCRIPTION	PACKAGING	PREPARATION	REFERENCE
White, whole wheat, rye, graham, semolina, soy, corn meal	12 oz to 25 lb bags	Good for use in baking	Stone Buhr
Cornmeal, white or cracked wheat flour	#10 cans	Good for use in baking	Survival Supply Ready Reserve
Freeze Dried Meats, Jerky, Meat Spreads, and Fish			
Chicken salad spread	4 person pouch	Ready to spread	Dri-Lite
Beef jerky	Individual pkts	Ready to eat	Stow-a-way
Freeze dried beef and pork patties	1 person pouch	Soak in boiling water; may be fried lightly after reconstitution	Survival Supply MRE's
Freeze dried beef, chicken and sausage, beef jerky	2 to 16 oz pkgs	Jerky is ready to eat; freeze dried meats need presoaking and minimal cooking	Dri-Lite
Freeze dried beef, chicken, meatballs, turkey and sausage. Canned bacon, bacon bars, beef jerky, pepperoni sticks	2 to 4 person servings	Soak in boiling water; may be fried lightly after reconstitution. Some are ready to eat.	Survival Supply Wee Pak
Freeze dried chicken or tuna salad	2 person pouch	Add cold water and soak	Survival Supply Wee Pak
Freeze dried tuna, ham, rib eye steak and steak pieces	#10 cans	Presoaking and minimal cooking	Mountain House
Canned bacon	6.4 oz can (9 to 12 servings/can)	Precooked; soak and heat	Westland-Trail Foods

DESCRIPTION	PACKAGING	PREPARATION	REFERENCE
Bacon or beef meat bars	2 oz pkgs	Ready to eat	Mountain House
Freeze dried beef or chicken	3 oz bag	Soak in hot water	Richmoor
Wine beef jerky	1 person pouch	Ready to eat	Richmoor
Freeze dried sausage patties	3 oz pkg	Soak in hot water; may be fried lightly after reconstitution	Mountain House
Beef jerky or sausage sticks	Individual pkts	Ready to eat	Mountain House
Freeze dried chicken, shrimp, tuna, clams	2 person pouch or 3 to 4 lb bulk	Add hot or cold water	Alpine Aire

Fruits

DESCRIPTION	PACKAGING	PREPARATION	REFERENCE
Applesauce, banana chips, apple slices, fruit cocktail, freeze dried strawberries or peaches, fruit mix, pineapple	2 or 4 person pouch	Eat as is or add cold water and soak	Dri-Lite
Banana chips, papaya, pineapple, coconut	11 to 17 lb bags; coconut in ½ to 1 lb bags	Ready to eat	Pavo
Low moisture apples, applesauce, banana chips, blueberry and raspberry flavored apples, fruit mix, prunes, date pieces, raisins	#2½ and #10 cans	Ready to eat or soak in water or heat to rehydrate	Perma Pak
Freeze dried peaches, pears, and mixed fruits	2 person pouch	Soak in cold water	Survival Supply MRE's

DESCRIPTION	PACKAGING	PREPARATION	REFERENCE
Apricot slices, apple slices, banana slices, applesauce, peach slices, raisins, prunes, fruit cocktail, date pieces	#2½ or #10 cans; some in 2 to 4 person pouches	Eat as is or soak in water to rehydrate	Survival Supply Ready Reserve
Applesauce, fruit salad with gelatin	2 person pouch	Add cold water	Survival Supply Wee Pak
Apricot, peach, or pear halves	4 person pouch	Ready to eat or rehydrate	Survival Supply Wee Pak
Banana chips, strawberries, peaches, fruit mix	#10 cans or 3 person pouch	Ready to eat or rehydrate	Mountain House
Prunes, apples, pears, apricots, peaches, dates	#10 cans or 8 oz can or poly bag	Ready to eat or rehydrate	Bernard
Banana chips, apple chips, applesauce, pineapple chunks	2 or 4 person pouch	Ready to eat or rehydrate	Richmoor
Applesauce, apple slices or pieces, apricots, bananas, peaches, dates, prunes, grapes, fruit mix	4 person pouch or #10 can	Ready to eat or rehydrate	Stow-a-way
Apples, apricots, dates, figs, prunes, pineapple, raisins	4 oz to 1 lb pkg or 5 lb bags	Ready to eat or rehydrate	Timber Crest Farms
Apples, apricots, figs, mango, papaya, pear, peach, pineapple	4 to 12 oz pkgs	Ready to eat or rehydrate	Alpine Aire
Freeze dried strawberries, blueberries, raspberries; peach, apple, and blueberry flakes	1 to 2 person pouch; flakes available in bulk	Soak in cold water	Alpine Aire

DESCRIPTION	PACKAGING	PREPARATION	REFERENCE
	Grains, Rice, and Pastas		
Brown rice, barley	32 to 34 oz bags	Moderately long cooking time	Stone Buhr
Barley, white, brown and basmati rice, buckwheat groats, corn, millet, rye, popcorn, wheat, oat groats, triticale	2 lb cello bags or 50 lb bags	Most require grinding or long cooking time; can be sprouted	Arrowhead Mills
Barley, rice	#10 cans	Moderately long cooking time	Perma Pak
Barley, bulgur, rye, brown and white rice, wheat, popcorn	#10 cans; some available in 35 to 37 lb buckets	Moderately long cooking time	Stow-a-way
White rice, rolled oats, wheat, macaroni	#10 cans	Moderately long cooking time	Survival Supply Ready Reserve
Barley, millet, wheat, rye, oat, and buckwheat groats, brown rice	1 to 2 lb pkgs; rice in 5 lb pkg	Moderately long cooking time	Pavo
Freeze dried or pre-cooked brown, wild or basmati rice, barley	3 person pouch (barley, brown, wild and basmati rice also in 4 lb bulk)	Add hot water and soak or cook a short time	Alpine Aire
Rice or egg noodles	Individual size perforated bag	Boil in bag 5 minutes	Smoky Canyon
Rice or egg noodles	Individual size perforated bag	Boil in bag 5 minutes	Yurika

DESCRIPTION	PACKAGING	PREPARATION	REFERENCE
Spaghetti, macaroni, ribbons, rosmarini	12 oz pkg	Boil 5 to 10 minutes	Yurika
White and wild rice combination	Individual size perforated bag	Boil in bag 5 minutes	Chef-to-go
Macaroni	#10 can	Boil a short time	Stow-a- way
Whole wheat macaroni	9 person pkg	Soak 10 minutes in boiling water	Alpine Aire
Macaroni	#10 can	Boil 10 minutes	Perma Pak
Meatless and Vegetarian Products and Entrees			
Vegetarian fish cakes	#10 can or 7½ to 22½ oz can	Soak in boiling water	Bernard
Textured vegetable protein (TVP) bacon, beef, chicken, ham, hamburger bits, granules and chunks	#10 cans	Short to moderate cooking time	Stow-a-way
TVP bacon, beef, ham and chicken	#2½ or #10 cans	Short to moderate cooking time	Perma Pak
Freeze dried textured soy protein in beef, ham and chicken flavor	#10 cans	Short cooking time	Stow-a- way
TVP bacon chips	#5 cans	Short to moderate cooking time	Bernard
TVP beef, chicken, ham or bacon	#2½ or #10 cans	Short to moderate cooking time	Survival Supply Ready Reserve

DESCRIPTION	PACKAGING	PREPARATION	REFERENCE
Beans in tomato sauce and applesauce	4.5 oz retort	Place in boiling water for 5 minutes	Survival Supply MRE's
Macaroni and cheese, Spanish style rice	#2½ cans	Short cooking time	Perma Pak
Chili, cheese-nut casserole, sesame burger mix	2 or 4 person pouch	Add boiling water and soak	Alpine Aire
Chili, vegetable pilaf, stew, spaghetti, mac 'n cheese, pasta and vegetables, quiche, curry, fettuccini	2 or 4 person pouch	Cook a short time with water	Dri-Lite
Vegetable stew, Oriental rice and herbs	4 person pouch	Cook a short time with water	Stow-a-way
Pasta with cheese and vegetables, spaghetti, pasta stews, rice pilaf, mac 'n cheese, couscous, hummus	2 or 4 person pouch	Add boiling water and soak	Alpine Aire
Canned meat substitutes, packaged soy and grain meat substitutes	10 to 50 oz cans or pkgs	Mix with water and cook or heat	Worthington Foods
Spaghetti, sloppy joe, chili, beef casserole, lasagne, stroganoff, mac 'n cheese, chow mein, beef noodle or chicken noodle stew, sweet and sour pork, Spanish rice	#10 cans, 12 to 22 oz cans or 3 to 7 oz cans	Add water and cook a short time	Bernard
Tofu	Hermetically sealed 10½ oz pkg	Use like regular tofu	Morinaga Foods

DESCRIPTION	PACKAGING	PREPARATION	REFERENCE
Nut Butters			
Peanut butter mix	4 oz pouch	Mix with oil or water	Richmoor
Peanut butter spread	4 person pouch	Ready to spread	Dri-Lite
Creamy or chunky peanut butter	12 to 28 oz bag, or 40 lbs	Ready to spread	Arrowhead Mills
Peanut butter powder	#2½ or #10 can or 6 person pouch	Mix with oil or water	Survival Supply Ready Reserve
Peanut butter powder	#2½ can	Mix with oil or water	Perma Pak
Peanut butter powder	4 person pouch	Mix with oil or water	Dri-Lite
Peanut butter powder	4 person pouch or #10 can	Mix with oil or water	Stow-a-way
Potatoes			
Hash browns	2 to 4 person pouch	Soak in boiling water and fry	Survival Supply Wee Pak
Potatoes with cheddar and chives	2 person pouch	Add boiling water	Alpine Aire
Potato flakes	4 person pouch	Add boiling water	Alpine Aire
Mashed potato mix	#10 can	Add boiling water	R.T. French
Plain mashed, au gratin	2 or 4 person pouch	Add boiling water	Dri-Lite
Mashed potato mix	#10 can	Add boiling water	Perma Pak
Hash browns	2 person pouch or #10 can	Soak in boiling water and fry	Mountain House

DESCRIPTION	PACKAGING	PREPARATION	REFERENCE
Hash browns (plain or O'Brien with bell pepper)	2 or 4 person pouch	Soak in boiling water and fry	Richmoor
Hash browns, mashed potatoes with milk	2 or 4 person pouch	Soak hash browns in water and fry; add boiling water to mashed potatoes	Stow-a-way
Mashed potato mix	2 oz or 2 lb bag	Add boiling water	Yurika
Potato granules, pieces and slices	#2½ or #10 cans	Add boiling water	Survival Supply Ready Reserve
Sauces, Dressings, and Syrups			
Maple syrup mix	2 or 4 person pkg	Add warm water	Dri-Lite
Maple syrup	4 person pouch	Ready to use	Richmoor
Maple syrup mix	4 person pouch	Add hot water	Stow-a-way
Maple syrup mix	2 or 4 person pouch	Add hot water	Survival Supply Wee Pak
Maple syrup granules or liquid	1 tsp pouch, 1½ to 2½ oz pouch or bulk	Add warm water to granules or sprinkle as a sweetener; liquid is ready to use	Alpine Aire
Tomato powder	#2½ or #10 can	Add water or oil	Perma Pak
Tomato crystals	4 person pouch	Mix with water	Stow-a-way
Tomato crystals	4 oz pouch	Mix with water	Richmoor
Tomato powder	3 to 4 oz pkg or by the pound	Mix with water	Alpine Aire

DESCRIPTION	PACKAGING	PREPARATION	REFERENCE
Tamari powder	3 to 4 oz pkg or by the pound	Mix with water	Alpine Aire
Mayonnaise powder mix	#10 can	Add water, oil and vinegar	Bernard
Hollandaise, Bearnaise, white, cream, Creole, sweet and sour sauce mix	#5 cans or 6½ to 8 oz cans	Add water and cook a short time; add tomato product to Creole; add pineapple to sweet and sour	Bernard
Spaghetti, barbecue, taco, chili, au jus, enchilada	16 to 20 oz can or #10 can	Add water and cook with other ingredients	Bernard
Soups and Bouillon			
Soup mix	2 lb pkg	Add hot water	Yurika
Variety of soup mixes and ramen	2 or 4 person pouch	Add boiling water or cook a short time	Alpine Aire
Potato-corn chowder	2 person pouch	Add water and cook a short time	Dri-Lite
Meatless chicken noodle, beef vegetable, rice, chowder, bean, stew and chili	19 oz cans	Heat and serve	Worthington
Variety of soup mixes	1½ oz pkg	Mix with boiling water	Red Wagon
Beef bouillon, vegetable noodle soup	#10 and #2½ can, respectively	Add boiling water or cook a short time	Perma Pak
Beef or chicken soup base, vegetable noodle soup	#2½ cans; vegetable soup in 4 person pouch	Add boiling water	Survival Supply Ready Reserve

DESCRIPTION	PACKAGING	PREPARATION	REFERENCE
Wide variety of soup mixes	16 to 32 oz poly bags or cans and #10 cans	Add water and cook a variable length of time	Bernard
Beef, chicken, and vegetable minestrone mix	4 person pouch	Add water and cook a short time	Stow-a-way
Beef or chicken bouillon	#10 can	Add boiling water	Stow-a-way
Tomato, chicken, onion, mushroom, minestrone, split pea, vegetable, cheese, lentil soup mix	2 person pouch	Add water and cook a short time	Hain Pure Food
Clam chowder, seafood chowder, lentil, mushroom, minestrone, tomato vegetable, chicken noodle, cream of chicken	2 or 4 person pouch	Add water and cook a short time	Survival Supply Wee Pak

Snacks

DESCRIPTION	PACKAGING	PREPARATION	REFERENCE
Carob bridge mix, carob peanuts, carob raisins	15 to 25 lb bag	Ready to eat	Pavo
Fruit pemmican bars, fruit leathers, chewy fruit, granola bars, fruit bars	Individual pkg	Ready to eat	Alpine Aire
Wha Guru bars, trail brunch, fruit chews	Individual pkg	Ready to eat	Richmoor
Gorp	2 person pouch	Ready to eat	Richmoor
Nut and chocolate mix	#10 cans or 2 person pouch	Ready to eat	Mountain House

DESCRIPTION	PACKAGING	PREPARATION	REFERENCE
Gorp, fruit and nut mix	2 person pouch	Ready to eat	Dri-Lite
Chocolate bar, trail cookies, fruit leather	4 person pouch	Ready to eat	Dri-Lite
Gorp, oatmeal cookies, fruit bars, granola bars, peanut butter bars	2 to 4 person pouch	Ready to eat	Survival Supply Wee Pak
Vegetables			
Peas, corn, green beans, carrots, peas and carrots, Sierra salad (gelatin and vegetables)	2 or 4 person pouch	Add boiling water or cook a short time	Dri- Lite
Cabbage, onions, green beans, carrots, peas, potato dices and slices, corn, celery	#2½ and #10 cans	Moderate cooking time	Perma Pak
Peas, green beans, corn	2 to 3 person pouch or #10 can	Minimal cooking time	Mountain House
Peas, carrots, green or red pepper, mixed vegetables, celery, onions, potato dices	8 oz poly bag	Soak in boiling water or cook a short time	Bernard
Corn, peas, green beans, carrots and peas	2 or 4 person pouch	Soak in boiling water or cook a short time	Richmoor
Potato dices, onion slices, carrots, peas, green beans, corn, spinach, beets, bell pepper, celery, cabbage	4 person pouch or #10 can	Add boiling water or cook a short time	Stow-a-way

DESCRIPTION	PACKAGING	PREPARATION	REFERENCE
Freeze dried and dehydrated peas, corn, carrots, mushrooms, sweet pepper combination, celery, onions, tomato, cabbage, spinach	2 or 4 person pouch or bulk	Add boiling water or cook a short time	Alpine Aire
Carrots, corn, green beans, mixed vegetables, peas, creamed spinach, lima beans	2 or 4 person pouch	Add boiling water or cook a short time	Survival Supply Wee Pak
Celery, carrots, corn, green peas, green beans, diced onions, green pepper, salad blend, cabbage, soup/stew blend	#2½ or #10 cans; some available in 2 or 4 person pouch	Add boiling water or cook a short time	Survival Supply Ready Reserve

Chapter 5

Stoves and Fuel

"Courts and camps are the only places to learn the world in."

Philip Dormer Stanhope, Earl of Chesterfield
Letter to his son, October, 1747

WHEN PLANNING THE TYPE of stove to buy for an expedition, major factors to consider include the type of fuel shipped to or available in the country of destination, stove durability, ease of starting and operation, BTU* output, burning time, maintenance, weight and size. Low cost cannot be justified if the stove becomes inoperable during the expedition due to its inability to meet the heavy demands placed on it. While many other needs in camp can be filled with improvisation, stoves are a life-link to nutrition, water supplies and survival. Don't scrimp!

*British Thermal Unit: the amount of heat necessary to raise the temperature of 1 pound of water 1°F.

Several different stove types for one expedition may be desirable, such as larger, heavier stoves for use in the lower, main camps, and lighter, easy to use stoves for use in high altitude or in distant camps.

Do not overlook the possibility of purchasing a large camp stove in the country of destination. Many areas have developed ingenious stoves which work well on locally available fuel. By obtaining them in the county of destination, shipping is avoided. Although procurement of stoves should not be left as the last thing to do before heading for high camp, obtaining one or two good local stoves may be helpful in augmenting one's own supply of stoves or providing extras in case of loss or breakdown of other stoves. Third world kitchens depend on such stoves and the place to look for them is in the local marketplace.

General Considerations

- Keep the stoves clean and fill the fuel tanks before each use, when the stoves are cool.
- Let the stoves cool before releasing pressure and opening the fuel chamber.
- Release pressure in the fuel tanks or drain the tanks before storage and travel to help prevent leaks.
- "Self-pressurized" stoves may need to be pumped with a mini-pump to increase efficiency.

Stove Comparison and Information Chart

The following stove comparison and information chart should help in deciding which stove(s) will best suit one's needs. The list is not all-inclusive, but provides information on most of the popular, easily available, time-tested camping stoves.

STOVE BRAND & MODEL	FUEL	WEIGHT & SIZE (without fuel)	ADVANTAGES & DISADVANTAGES	ACCESSORIES & REPAIRS	COST*
MSR X-GK	Leaded or unleaded automotive fuel, #1 stove fuel, kerosene, aviation fuel, Stoddard solvent	1 lb with pump Empty fuel flask in 22 fl oz size is 4.5 oz Maintenance kit, 1 oz	Excellent in cold, good in wind. Has integral sparker so no matches needed. Fairly stable when flask is attached. Adjustable flame. Easy to clean and repair in the field. One year limited warranty. Boils 1 qt of water in 3½ min. Needs to be primed when using kerosene as fuel. Fair pot stability. Burns up to 2 hours on high. Compact.	Wind screen, heat reflector, fuel flask, repair tools. Maintenance kit available. Built-in sparker.	High
MSR Firefly	White gas	15 oz. with pump 2¼ x 6 x 4½ in.	Excellent in cold. Fairly stable; can be suspended when cooking on ground is difficult. Adjustable flame. Easy to clean and repair. Burns 1½ hours on high; boils 1 qt. water in 3 min. Must be primed. Compact.	Maintenance kit available. Fuel flask.	Moderate
MSR Whisperlite	White gas	12 oz. 4½ x 6 in.	Fairly stable. Runs quietly. Very compact. Runs well in cold weather. Boils 1 qt. of water in 4½ min. Must be primed.	Windscreen, reflector. Maintenance kit available.	Low to moderate

STOVE BRAND & MODEL	FUEL	WEIGHT & SIZE (without fuel)	ADVANTAGES & DISADVANTAGES	ACCESSORIES & REPAIRS	COST*
MSR Internationale	Kerosene or white gas	13.3 oz 3¾ x 5¼ in.	Fairly stable when fuel flask is attached, good in cold and wind, adjustable flame, easy to clean and repair, compact; must change jets if fuel type is switched.	Windscreen, reflector, gasoline and kerosene jets, jet tool cleaning tool, priming container. Maintenance kit available.	Moderate
Coleman three burner deluxe gas camp stove 426E499	White gas	19 lbs. 28½ x 13¾ x 6¼ in.	Adjustable flame, stable, good in wind, durable. 25,800 BTU output. Burns 2 hours on high. Heavy, need to take extra generators, cumbersome to clean.	Aluminum stand, chef trays, oven, griddle.	High. Oven: low
Coleman two burner deluxe gas stove 413H499	White gas	15 lbs. 23¼ x 14¾ x 7¼ in.	Adjustable flame, good in wind, stable, durable. Burns 2 hours on high. 25,600 BTU output. Heavy; need to take extra generators, cumbersome to clean.	Aluminum stand, chef tray, oven, griddle.	Moderate
Coleman two burner standard gas stove 425F499	White gas	11 lbs. 19 x 12¼ x 6 in.	Adjustable flame, stable, good in wind, durable. Burns 2 hours on high. 18,700 BTU output. Heavy, need to take extra generators, cumbersome to clean.	Aluminum stand, chef tray, oven, griddle.	Low to moderate

STOVE BRAND & MODEL	FUEL	WEIGHT & SIZE (without fuel)	ADVANTAGES & DISADVANTAGES	ACCESSORIES & REPAIRS	COST*
Coleman Sportster II 508-700	White gas	3½ lbs. with case	Lights easily, burns well in wind, burns 1¾ hour on high. 8,500 BTU output. Flame is not adjustable.	Carrying case	Low
Coleman Peak I Multifuel	Coleman fuel, kerosene, jet fuel, unleaded auto fuel, white gas	18.7 oz. 5¼ x 4½ in.	Burns 1½ to 2 hours on high. Boils 1 qt. water in 3½ to 4½ min. 8,000 BTU output.	Fuel tip cleaner, wind screen, pot support, built-in pump	Moderate
Coleman Peak I	White gas	28.5 oz. 6 x 4½ in.	Good in cold weather, stable, adjustable flame, built-in cleaning needle and integral windscreen. Boils 1 qt. in 4½ min. 8,500 BTU output. Burns 70 min. on high. May need to prime in very cold temperatures.	Built-in pressure pump and cleaning needle.	Low
Coleman deluxe two burner propane stove 5410A700	Propane	11 lbs. 21½ x 13½ x 4½ in.	Stable, good in wind, durable, adjustable flame, can be used on a bulk propane system, easy to clean. 20,000 BTU output with both burners on high. Must carry 16.4 or 14.1 oz. propane cartridges or refillable bulk system.		Moderate

STOVE BRAND & MODEL	FUEL	WEIGHT & SIZE (without fuel)	ADVANTAGES & DISADVANTAGES	ACCESSORIES & REPAIRS	COST*
Optimus 111 Hiker	Kerosene, white gas, alcohol	54 oz. 7 x 7 x 4 in.	Stable, good in wind and cold, built-in cleaning needle, durable. Burns 1⅓ hour on high. Must be primed.	Comes with a wrench for repairs in the field.	High
Optimus 123R Climber or Svea	White gas	19½ oz. 3¾ x 5 in.	Aluminum cover acts as a pot, built- in cleaning needle, good at altitude, compact. Burns 75 min. on high. 4,700 BTU/hr output. Boils 1 qt. of water in 7 min. Durable. Needs windscreen or efficiency is decreased. May need to use mini-pump to increase efficiency. Not too stable or good in cold. Must be primed.	Pot supports, windshield, mini-pump is available. The 123R comes without pots.	Low to moderate
Optimus 324 Rider	White gas	26 oz. 4¾ x 4½ in.	"Quick-lighter" built in for easy lighting, built-in cleaning needle. Burns 45 min. on high. Boils 1 qt. water in 5 min. Not very stable.		Moderate

STOVE BRAND & MODEL	FUEL	WEIGHT & SIZE (without fuel)	ADVANTAGES & DISADVANTAGES	ACCESSORIES & REPAIRS	COST*
Optimus 8R Hunter	White gas	21 oz. 5 x 5 x 3 in.	Built-in cleaning needle, durable case, good stability. Burns 50 min. on high. 3,300 BTU/hr. output. Boils 1 qt. of water in 12 min. Not too good in cold, must be primed, pot stability not too good. Mini-pump can increase efficiency.	Mini-pump available.	Low to moderate
Optimus 00 Camper	Kerosene	25 oz. 7½ x 5 in.	Built-in windshield, fairly stable, durable, compact, good in cold. Burns 120 min. on high. 6,000 BTU/hr. output. Boils 1 qt. water in 8½ min. Can leak if packed with fuel in the tank. Must be primed.	Repair and cleaning accessories provided.	Moderate
Optimus 199 Ranger	White gas, kerosene, alcohol	32 oz. 5 x 5 x 4 in.	Lid acts as a pot, stable, built-in cleaning needle. 8,500 BTU/hr. output. Burns up to ½ hour on high. Boils 1 qt. water in 5½ min. with kerosene. Needs windshield, must be primed, may need mini-pump to increase efficiency.	Windshield, pot handle, mini-pump provided.	Moderate

STOVE BRAND & MODEL	FUEL	WEIGHT & SIZE (without fuel)	ADVANTAGES & DISADVANTAGES	ACCESSORIES & REPAIRS	COST*
Optimus 81 Trapper	Alcohol	34 oz. 8 x 4½ in.	Adjustable burner, no need for preheating, works at high altitude and cold. 4,000 BTU/hr. output. Boils 1 qt. water in 9 min. Low heat output.	Two pots, frying pan, windshield, pot handle, scoop and carrying strap provided.	Moderate
Camping Gaz International C-206 Bleuet	Butane	12 oz. 3¾ x 7½ in. C-206 cartridge – 10¼ oz.	Cartridges are available in 120 countries, no priming or pumping, very easy to operate. Boils 1 qt. of water in 9 min. Burns 2½ hours on high. Must carry out cartridges. Base is not too stable. Cartridges must be kept above 30°F	Windshield, grid to stabilize large pots, base.	Low
Camping Gaz International Globetrotter	Butane	16 oz. including cooking set. GT-106 cartridge – 5¾ oz.	Cartridges are available in 120 countries, no priming or pumping, very easy to operate. Boils 1 pint of water in 4½ min. Burns 1¼ hour on high. Must carry out cartridges. Base not too stable. Cartridges must be kept above 30°F	Fold-away pan supports, windshield, 2 one- pint pots, handle and carrying strap provided.	Low

STOVE BRAND & MODEL	FUEL	WEIGHT & SIZE (without fuel)	ADVANTAGES & DISADVANTAGES	ACCESSORIES & REPAIRS	COST*
Camping Gaz International Instaflam	Butane	21 oz. Uses C-206 cartridge	See C-206 Bleuet. Has Piezo electric ignition.	Plastic cover provides protection.	Moderate
EPIgas Deluxe Picnicker 53004	Propane	Uses cartridge, 165 gms.	Lightweight; self-sealing removable cartridge. Good at high altitude and low temperature.	Fold-away pan supports, lid doubles as a windshield, stainless steel carry tin, base, utensil with detachable handle.	Low
EPIgas Picnicker 53001	Propane	Cartridge, 165 gms.	Lightweight; self-sealing removable cartridge.	Built-in wind shield, pan supports and safety ring.	Low
EPIgas Backpacker 53009	Propane	Cartridge, 165 gms.	Lightweight; self-sealing removable cartridge.	Fold-away pan supports, base, windshield, pot, frying pan and handle.	Low

Cost: Low – $16-39; Moderate – $40-69; High – $70 to 100.

FUELS

General Considerations

- Keep fuel bottles labeled and in a separate area from stoves or from food containers with which they may become confused.
- "Gasoline" stoves burn white gas, not automobile gasoline (except the MSR X-GK and Coleman Peak I Multifuel stoves; unleaded gasoline recommended).
- Under winter conditions in which water will have to be obtained by melting snow or ice, allow 2 liters of fuel per person per week for melting.
- Use pot lids to help conserve heat, to prevent too rapid dehydration of the food during cooking, to help prevent scorching, and to conserve fuel. Presoaking foods can decrease cooking time. Also, after cooking, turn off the flame, cover the pot and allow it to sit 10 minutes before serving to complete cooking without the use of fuel.
- Use a pressure cooker at higher altitudes to cook foods faster and conserve fuel.
- Always use a funnel filter when filling stoves to prevent particulate matter from entering the fuel tank.
- Use metal or plastic bottles specially designed to hold fuel to prevent leakage or reaction of the fuel with the container.
- Do not cook with gasoline in a closed tent as an explosive atmosphere might result. If weather conditions prevent using a gas stove outside, start the stove outside of the tent, then move the stove and regulated flame into the tent and leave a flap or window open for ventilation.
- Never fill a gas stove in the tent, in the presence of stoves that are running, or near any other open flame source.
- Make sure the stove is in a stable position to prevent spillage of food or fuel.

- Carbon monoxide is a colorless, tasteless, and odorless gas produced by the incomplete combustion of certain fuels. Carbon monoxide destroys the abiltiy of red blood cells to carry oxygen adequately. Its production is usually the result of faulty equipment, improper use of equipment or inadequate ventilation. Follow instructions for stove and fuel usage and always provide adequate ventilation. Small and cheap carbon monoxide monitors are available from most fixed base operators, facilities that service privately owned airplanes. Also see Appendix VII for the supplier. Such monitors are a sure sign of dangerous carbon monoxide buildup within a cook tent, for example.

Fuel Comparisons

- White gasoline (not automotive fuel) is a highly combustible fuel with a high heat output. Spilled fuel evaporates easily and does not leave a smelly residue. Gas stoves require priming, but can be primed with their own fuel. Gas stoves are easy to light. The stove must be insulated from snow or cold if it is a self-pressurizing variety. Fuel is available in the United States, but may be difficult to obtain outside the U.S.

- Kerosene is a less combustible fuel that also produces a high heat output. Spilled fuel does not easily ignite, but it leaves an oily, smelly area where spilled. Kerosene stoves are more complicated to light than white gas stoves and require priming with alcohol, white gas or gel-type "fire ribbon". Kerosene stoves can sit directly on the snow. Kerosene generally is available throughout the world.

- Butane is contained in metal cartridges that are expensive and must be packed out when empty. Some cartridges cannot be changed until completely empty. There is no fuel to spill. No priming is required for stoves and the flame immediately has maximum heat output, although butane has a lower heat output than many other fuels. Fuel cartridges should be above freezing for maximum operation. Cartridges may be difficult to obtain in some countries outside of the U.S. and Europe.

- Alcohol evaporates readily and dries without a lingering smell or residue. Spilled fuel is quite flammable. No priming is required but alcohol has a low heat output and is inefficient in cold weather. Fuel is available in most countries.

- Propane is available in cartridges or can be used as a bulk system with several stoves running off one large tank. Good heat output is obtained with propane. Propane leaks produce a highly combustible atmosphere in an enclosed area. Use of large tanks is nearly prohibitive due to size and weight and refills are difficult to find except in the U.S. and foreign metropolitan areas. Propane could be a very useful fuel for a large research or outdoor camp in North America, where transport of tanks for refilling is possible.

- Automotive gasoline can be used in several stoves, but it is a highly combustible material and easily produces a volatile atmosphere. Extreme caution must be exercised if this fuel is used. Unleaded varieties are recommended to prevent lead contamination of the atmosphere and foods. It is generally available, even in very remote areas.

Chapter 6

Utensils and Equipment

"I took a kettle large and new, fit for the deed I had to do."
Lewis Carroll
THROUGH THE LOOKING GLASS

Many DIFFERENT COOKING and eating kits are commercially available. Provision boxes and mess kits, although compact, are usually too small or inconvenient from which to eat. Instead, a large, durable margarine tub, polycarbonate utensils and a 16 ounce capacity measuring cup for drinking make a lightweight, cheap, nearly indestructible mess kit that can be jammed into spare pack corners. Such utensils should not be shared or loaned to help prevent the spread of disease.

Many companies produce nesting, lightweight, convenient cooking sets, but most are for small groups from 1 to 4 persons. Most include a few miscellaneous, often unnecessary accessories, such as 8 ounce plastic cups or a set of eating utensils. Handles are usually collapsible, lids serve also as plates and a teapot of less than 1 liter capacity may be included. In general, one is paying for convenience of a matched set of nesting pans of small size. Although such sets are lightweight and easy to carry and may be useful at high altitude camps, they are of little benefit at larger, lower camps where large quantities of food must be prepared in more stable or heavy pans.

For quantity cookery, larger pots and pans that heat more evenly, have stable handles and are lined with non-stick surfaces are ideal. Because many meals are large but cooked over a small camp stove flame, the pot or pan should be relatively thick to prevent "hot spots" and scorching. Aluminum pans are lightweight even when thick and heat more evenly than stainless steel. The pans are going to become battered and stained no matter how hard one tries to keep them nice, so the increased weight and inferior cooking quality of stainless steel cannot be justified, since a camp pan must be chosen for its utility, not its looks. Non-stick coatings are recommended, as they greatly ease clean up and make cooking and frying much easier.

Long handles found on conventional cooking pans take up space in packing and on the stove and are easily snagged by cuffs, other pots and objects around the stove, thereby upsetting the pan. Riveted side handles or bail handles are more easily packed, allow for nesting of pans and form a more stable, easy to carry pot. Frying pans are an exception to this, as they are much easier and safer to use with a conventional handle and more stable than handleless frying pans used with pot tongs. Frying pans with folding handles are available, which make packing more convenient.

Each pan should have its own lid. Invariably, if the frying pan and a large pot share a lid, one will be cooking with both and need a lid for each. The extra weight and space taken up by a lid is more than justified by its use as a conserver of heat and fuel while cooking and a method of keeping food warm on the table. In some cases, billy can (bailed handle pots) lids are also used as frying pans along with a pot tong. These deep lids, when turned upside down over the top of a pot of boiling soup or liquid and covered with another lid or tin foil, serve well as warmers for breads or keep other foods warm until serving.

Enameled pots, although nice to look at and easy to keep clean, often are knocked about harshly enough to chip the enamel, which then causes a hard-to-clean spot and can flake off pieces of enamel into the food being prepared, and so are not recommended.

Compartmented plates and griddles are not recommended, as they rarely conform to the meal being prepared or eaten and can be hard to clean. The use of a second pot or pan and the use of a large deep bowl for eating is better.

Extra pie plates are very convenient for serving foods and make nice plates after an individual's personal eating bowl/plate becomes misplaced or hidden deep in the recesses of a tent.

A good source of frying pans and pots is the local discount store. A large selection of many brands, styles and sizes is available, so individual needs can almost always be met. Other sources include restaurant equipment supply houses and Army/Navy surplus stores or catalogs. Specialty camping stores have selections of camping utensils, but often at a premium, and the sets are usually only for small groups.

CLEANING EQUIPMENT

An important part of general camp hygiene is keeping cooking and eating utensils clean which helps prevent the spread of disease, spoilage of food and influx of vermin.

Each member of the expedition should be responsible for procurement, care and cleaning of his own individual cup, plate/bowl and utensils. This helps prevent loss and sharing of personal equipment and cuts down on the number of dishes to be washed by the cook or person designated to clean up after each meal. Most importantly, it helps prevent the spread of disease from one individual to the next.

Disposable materials for cleanup such as paper toweling are very convenient and help prevent the spread of disease because they are thrown away after use. However, they are expensive, must be packaged and shipped in large quantities and produce a large amount of refuse which must be burned or carried out. Although a supply of paper towels is necessary for certains jobs, for utensil and equipment clean up it is better to have reusable sponges and scouring pads and a supply of semi-disposable towels/wipes such as Handi-wipes.™ These should be used only for clean up of cooking pans and utensils (each person is urged to use his own sponge, scrubbers and wipes for personal utensil cleanup). Bring a large enough supply of sponge-scrubbers and wipes so that worn out materials can be replaced.

Three plastic dish pans serve as reservoirs for wash, rinse and disinfection water. These should not be used for other purposes such as personal bathing and washing clothes. Liquid and tablet forms of disinfectants can be obtained from restaurant supply houses. Alternately, 1 tablespoon of household bleach per gallon of rinse water may be used.

Dunk bags are mesh bags in which soiled dishes can be placed, secured and then "dunked" into a stream or other body of water to soak as an aid to cleaning. Utensils placed in a dunk bag should be thoroughly scraped first to help prevent contamination of the water with food particles. The dunk bag should be placed downstream from the area where water is collected for eating and drinking purposes.

A whisk broom and dust pan are very handy to have to clean out tent floors. A supply of cording such as clothesline or avalanche cord and clothes pins are indispensable for drying towels, wipes and laundry.

REPAIR EQUIPMENT

A general repair kit is necessary on an expedition. The following list is helpful from the cook's standpoint. Climbing members may want to add their own tools, or provide a separate climbing tool kit.

Pliers (needle nose and regular)
Ice pick
Screw drivers (various sizes of Phillips and flat-head)
Hammer
Coil of all-purpose wire
Sewing kit and awl (thread, needles, pins, safety pins, thimble)
Nail clippers

Glue
Disposable lighters
Stove repair kits for each type of stove
Patches of tent material for mending
Repair kits and extra valves for air mattresses
Roll of heavy duct or strapping tape

STOVE BASES AND SHOVELS

Stove bases provide a flat, stable surface on which to set the stoves to help prevent food and fuel spillage and to decrease the chance of stoves falling over, causing fire or damage to the stove. Sections of plywood are excellent stove bases and can be placed on snow platforms, piles of flat rocks or over other supporting structures.

One shovel (clearly marked) for every 8 to 10 people should be provided for latrine digging and maintenance and used for no other purposes. One grain scoop shovel or avalanche shovel (clearly marked) should be used for collection of snow for melting into drinking water and used for no other purpose. One or more additional grain scoop/avalanche shovels and ice saws should be provided if necessary for igloo building, snow cave digging, making tent platforms and other camp chores.

TABLES AND CHAIRS

Lightweight folding aluminum and canvas chairs and stools can be taken to provide comfortable rests for cooking, eating, planning, reading and resting. Folding and roll-up tables that are lightweight and sturdy come in sizes that can easily be carried by man or beast and are indispensable in the dining tent/shelter for meals, letter writing and meetings. In permanent camps, plywood suspended between rock supports, stacks of flat rocks, or empty packing cases can also be used for tables and chairs when more conventional sources have not been brought along.

LANTERNS

Nothing seems to be quite as comforting as the hiss and warm glow of a mantle lantern in a tent in a cold, far-away place. However, now lamps and lanterns run the gamut from candles to electric light bulbs powered by gas generators. Choosing the right light source for one's needs depends mostly on the type of energy source that provides the light. General considerations include:

- If mantle lanterns are used, be sure to take along plenty of spare mantles.
- Always filter fuel through a filtering funnel when filling the lantern.
- Carry a lantern parts kit which includes mantles, pump lubricant and generator wrench.
- The U.S. Army/Navy surplus has a large stock of batteries, flashlights, electric lanterns, carbide lamps, kerosene lanterns, candles and candle lanterns, headlamps and flares.
- Simple candle lanterns can be very convenient to use in your personal pack, especially in remote villages and trailheads, where electricity is provided for only a

few hours a day or is non-existent. They illuminate late-night forays to latrines and are excellent for reading.

• Points to consider when choosing which lantern type to take include fuel used and its availability, weight, candlepower, burning time, adjustability features, accessories and cost.

• As with stoves, several types and sizes of lanterns may be desirable to fit differing needs.

THERMOSES

The extra space and weight taken up by thermos bottles can be justified by the savings in fuel and ease of access to hot water. Several large thermoses (usually available in the country of destination) for use at base camp and advanced camps provide a readily available supply of hot water for beverages by only heating the water once. Convenience of a source of hot water promotes fluid intake and prevents fuel wastage by reheating.

CONTAINERS
Water Bottles

Personal preference is best for individual water bottles. The bottle should be durable, resistant to breakage and leakage, at least 1 liter in capacity and possibly insulated to retain heat or cold. Such insulation may be part of the bottle design, may be a jacket made specifically for such a purpose, or may be closed cell foam cut and taped around the bottle and lid. Additionally, a strap or piece of cord tied around the neck of the bottle and attached to the lid through a hole is very important to prevent loss of the lid. Metal bottles are not recommended due to possible reaction with certain water purification methods and chemicals. Also, metal bottles may be crushed or bent, are more expensive than polyethylene bottles, may weight more, and are not visible internally to make sure they are clean.

Fuel Bottles

Several companies produce aluminum bottles for fuel. They have leak-proof seals, come in several sizes, are low weight, durable and may include a pour spout for easy filling of stoves. Make sure the bottles are designed for fuel, as certain metals or finishes may react with fuel, and some plastics are decomposed by fuel. Nalgene makes 1 pint and 1 quart bottles for fuel in gasoline-impermeable nylon. U.S. Army/Navy Surplus has a wide variety of larger gas cans and heavy duty jerricans for fuel, as well as spouts, funnels and fuel filters.

Food Storage Bottles and Jars

Polycarbonate jars are produced in a wide range of sizes (1 to 32 ounce) and shapes. The jars and bottles are extremely impact resistant, even at freezing temperatures. Polyethylene jars and bottles are produced in many sizes and styles by many companies and are excellent for food storage.

Bulk Water Supply and Carriers

Plastic water storage/carrier bottles which fold flat for storage and shipment are extremely useful. Most have a handle for carrying and an open/close spout for pouring. Folding carriers are available in 1.5, 2.5 and 5 gallon sizes and accordion folding carriers are available in 4 and 6 quart capacities. Pillow-type flexible, nylon taffeta containers are available which have a spigot and hold about 3 gallons. A shower assembly can be obtained to convert the bag into a shower. Similar products in 2½ and 5 gallon sizes have an on/off showerhead and the water is heated by solar power to provide a warm shower. U.S. Army/Navy Surplus has a wide variety of canvas water buckets, wash basins and canvas water bags.

Reusable Plastic Food Tubes

Clear plastic tubes with a screw top are available which can be filled from the bottom and then closed with a clamp. They are excellent for paste type food, condiments, medicines and lotions.

Plastic Bags

A good supply of plastic bags is always useful. While dividing and repackaging food prior to departure, a heat-sealing device and bags can be most helpful. The divided portions can be given an air-tight seal in a very sturdy plastic bag. However, such a bag is difficult to reseal once opened.

A supply of twist-tie, fold-over or zip-lock plastic bags in a wide range of sizes is imperative. They serve all types of needs including food packages, pack liners, clothing storage, litter collection and waste disposal, emergency vapor barrier liners and many other uses. When bulk foods are divided, small portions can be placed in sealable plastic and labeled with felt markers as to contents, date, destination and instructions for cooking. Self- sealing freezer bags are most durable, although double bagging in thinner bags also works well.

Miscellaneous Containers

Drop-dispenser bottles in ½, 1 and 2 ounce sizes are very useful for priming stoves, dispensing condiments, lotions and liquid medications. Disposable droppers are also available for priming stoves and other activities requiring a small amount of liquid.

Snap cap shaker tops which fit on 35mm film canisters, available at most backpacking stores, can be indispensable for spice jars.

The local discount or drug stores also can provide a wide variety of containers for all types of storage from food to toiletries and medicines, and can be much cheaper than containers produced and sold by specialty companies. Be sure, however, that containers for fuels are approved for fuel, and are leakproof and durable.

GENERAL KITCHEN UTENSIL AND EQUIPMENT
(designed for 12 people)

- 2 2-burner stoves
- 2 3-burner stoves
- 6 1-burner, multi fuel stoves
- 4 plywood stove platforms
- 1 Coleman oven
- 6 20-cup coffee pots
- 6 10" frying pans with lids
- 2 20 quart pots with lids
- 4 10 quart pots with lids
- 6 6 quart pots with lids
- 6 4 quart pots with lids
- 6 2 quart pots with lids
- 2 8 quart pressure cookers
- 5 5 gallon collapsible water jugs
- 2 plastic funnel sets
- 10 wide-mouth food storage jars
- 10 plastic food containers with lids (nesting, various sizes)
- 2 sets plastic nesting mixing bowls
- 1 griddle
- 3 ladles
- 6 large serving spoons

- 3 strainer spoons
- 3 spatulas
- 2 paring knives
- 2 serrated knives
- 2 butcher knives
- 2 cutting boards
- 3 can openers
- 1 pair tongs
- 2 plastic 8 ounce measuring cups
- 4 aluminum pie plates
- 4 pot holders
- 2 pot grippers
- 1 strainer/collander
- 1 small kitchen scale
- 1 meat thermometer
- 1 candy thermometer
- 1 steaming rack
- 1 dozen disposable lighters
- 2 packages clothes pins (wooden or wire)
- 2 whisk brooms/dust pans
- 3 large plastic dishpans
- 2 quarts biodegradable soap
- 10 scrub sponges
- 24 disposable wipes

Chapter 7

Camp Hygiene

*H*YGIENE IS THE SELF-EMPLOYMENT of practices which preserve health and prevent disease, such as proper drinking, eating and body cleanliness habits. It is probably best for the main responsibility for camp hygiene to be given to one person, so uniformity of the job can exist and a maintenance routine can be established. In this manner, supervision of health aspects of campsites, water supplies, food and its preparation, waste disposal, washing facilities and insect and rodent control can be maintained.

TENT PLACEMENT

Ideally, the cooking and dining tent or shelter should be placed in a flat, easily accessible, well-drained area, preferably apart from the sleeping tents, downstream or 30 meters (100 feet) from the water source and well away from latrine and waste disposal areas.

WATER

In order to keep water supplies clean for oneself and those that come after, treat water as the precious commodity it is. Sources of water are public supply systems, surface water (lakes, rivers, streams and ponds), ground water (wells and springs), melted ice or snow, rain collected from catchment surfaces and distilled sea water. All sources mentioned above in all countries, except United States, Canadian, and European public supplies, should be presumed to be contaminated.

If a surface water source is flowing and non-frozen, water should be carried in containers from the water source upstream of any known contamination and used after treatment for cooking, drinking, washing and bathing. If possible, a shallow, accessible area of the water supply should be hollowed out and dammed up to aid in decreasing turbulance and allowing silt to settle out. Also, it is easier to bail water out of such a depression than to try to ladle water from shallow, running areas, because such activities increase turbidity of the water collected.

Ground water sources should be located so origins of contamination such as pit latrines cannot drain into them.

Rainwater must be collected from clean catchment surfaces (rooftops, tarps, plastic) into clean, covered containers.

Above the snowline on sunny days, large quantities of water can be melted from snow and ice by solar energy, thus sparing fuel. A depression is made in the snow and covered with a thick, dark plastic sheet. Snow is spread thinly over its surface and heat absorbed by the tarp melts the snow, which forms a pool of water in the depression. This water can be bailed into containers for use and the process repeated. Although attention is required, it can be worked into daily camp rituals or relegated to other members in camp on a rotational basis. Above 4,500 meters (15,000 feet), solar melting becomes less efficient as the snow tends to sublimate directly into water vapor.[1] All snow and ice should be considered contaminated as freezing does not kill many organisms.

In all instances, extreme care must be taken to prevent

recontamination after the water has been treated, unless the treatment has residual activity against reinfection. Water containers should never be used for other purposes and should be cleaned and checked frequently for leaks and other sources of contamination.

Contamination of Water

All backcountry water sources including those inside the United States should be considered contaminated, regardless of how cold and clear they may seem. Not only humans, but ranging domestic and wild animals can carry organisms pathogenic to humans and can infect otherwise remote sources of water. In addition, chemical pollution can occur due to previous waste disposal, soap impurities, mining or industry.

Travel brings susceptible persons into tropical or under-developed areas where gastointestinal infections are common hazards, especially giardiasis, amebiasis, shigellosis, typhoid fever and colibacillosis.[2] The most common means of transmission of intestinal diseases are the five F's: feces, fingers, flies, food and fluids.[3]

Avoid the use of ice, as freezing of contaminated water does not purify it. Moisture on the outside of bottles and cans can be contaminated and must be dried off before opening the can or bottle, although bottled and canned drink contents are usually safe. Fruits and vegetables must be thoroughly washed in treated water before cutting or peeling if eaten raw, or thoroughly cooked and still hot when eaten. Be careful to wash hands frequently with soap and water, especially before handling food and after visits to the latrine. Remember to wash one's face and brush one's teeth only in treated or boiled water.

Protozoa

Giardiasis or traveler's diarrhea is caused by *Giardia lamblia*, a one-celled animal that has an active, mobile stage and a cyst stage. Giardia lives as the mobile form in the upper small intestine and usually forms a cyst as it passes down the gastrointestinal tract, although both forms can be found in diarrheic stools. Fecal contamination of food and water with cysts is the mode of transmission. It can be transmitted by ingestion of water contamined by man, dogs, cats, sheep, beaver and cattle. Symptoms include diarrhea (without blood), stomach pain, nausea, "rotten egg" belches, flatulance, lassitude, dehydration and weight loss appearing one to four weeks after exposure. The disease responds well to metronidazole. Boiling, filtration or iodination are effective in killing the cysts, but ordinary chlorination of water does not kill the cysts.[4] [5]

Amebic dysentery is caused by *Entamoeba histolytica* and produces a persistent diarrhea, abdominal discomfort and cramps, dehydration and bloody stools (dysentery). The organism can also invade other organs such as the liver and cause an accompanying fever and serious illness. The organism occurs in an active stage and several pre-cyst and cystic stages. The active form lives in the large intestine and forms a cyst before stool is passed or shortly thereafter. These cysts are taken in with fecally contaminated food and water. It is common in non-human primates, man and dog. The disease may become very debilitating, especially when liver involvement and septicemia occur. Metronidazole can be used for treatment.[6] Both the mobile and encysted stages succumb to iodination, filtration or proper boiling of water, but ordinary chlorination may not kill the cyst stage.

Bacteria

Cholera is caused by the bacterium *Vibrio cholerae* which is spread by ingesting contaminated water. Signs include a frequent, copious, watery, gray stool without blood and severe, rapid dehydration. A vaccine is available, but only gives limited protection. Treatment includes vigorous fluid therapy and tetracycline.

The bacteria *Escherichia coli* causes colibacillosis, a diarrheal disease most commonly transmitted by fecal contamination of food, water and inanimate objects. Treatment consists of fluid therapy and oral antibiotics to which the organism is susceptible.

Bacillary dysentery or shigellosis is caused by the bacterium *Shigella dysenteriae*. Symptoms include diarrhea with blood and mucus, abdominal cramps, fever and dehydration. The disease is spread by fecal contamination of food, water and inanimate objects. Broad spectrum antibiotics and fluid therapy are used for treatment.

Typhoid fever, caused by *Salmonella typhi*, causes fever, diarrhea or constipation, dehydration and abdominal distention. It is passed by fecal contamination of food and water. Treatment includes fluid therapy with the use of antibiotics reserved only for cases of continued fever and septicemia.[7] A typhoid vaccine is used to prevent the disease.

Viruses

The disease commonly referred to as "traveler's diarrhea" or "turista" is often caused by a parvo virus which is passed by fecal contamination of food and water, or by fecal-oral contact. Signs include diarrhea, vomiting, abdominal pain, nausea, occasional fever and dehydration. Treatment is aimed at rehydration through fluid therapy and the use of antispasmodics. It is a self-limiting disease.

Hepatitis A, also known as infectious hepatitis, is passed by food and water contaminated by feces. There is an abrupt onset of fever, inappetence, abdominal pain and possibly jaundice. No specific treatment is available, but passive immunity with immune serum globulin may be protective for about 2 months.

Water Purification

Water of unsure purity can be treated effectively chemically, through a filter, and by boiling. Water treated chemically has the advantage over other methods of residual protection against recontamination. Water cleaned through filters or by boiling has no such residual protection and must be placed in clean containers and guarded carefully against subsequent recontamination.

Chemical Treatment

Iodine tablets such as Potable Aqua® contain 16.7% tetraglycine hydroperiodide and are a germicidal treatment for water. Recommended use is 1 tablet per quart or liter of water; wait 3 minutes, shake well, then slightly loosen the cap and allow the iodinated water to contact the threads of the cap. Wait 10 more minutes before drinking or adding flavored drink mixes to the water. If the water is very cold, wait 20 minutes. If the water contains organic material or is very cloudy, use 2 tablets and wait 20 minutes. When iodinated water is heated, it becomes cloudy and brown and the free iodine can be tasted, which may be unpleasant to some people. The tablets must be fresh and be stored properly. The tablets should not be used on a long-term basis. The cost and weight of such treatment is minimal.

Crystalline iodine can be used as an effective and inexpensive water treatment. In a 1 ounce bottle, place 0.25 ounces (7 grams) of crystalline iodine. Fill the bottle with water, shake and let stand 1 hour. Use 1 capful per quart or liter of water, allowing the treated water to rinse the threads of the cap. Let stand 20 minutes before drinking or adding drink mixes. If the water is very cold or cloudy, use 2 capfuls and let stand 40 minutes. This treatment has the same undesirable effects on appearance and taste of the water as iodine tablets, but is germicidal. Some commercially prepared bottles, such as Polar Pure®, are available which treat 2,000 quarts of water. Iodine crystals are trapped in a specially designed bottle and a thermometer is available to determine temperature and dosages for water treatment.

Five drops of 2% tincture of iodine can be used per quart or liter of water for treatment. The threads of the cap are rinsed with the treated water and the mixture allowed to stand 30 minutes before use. If water is cold or cloudy, wait 60 minutes. (Do not mix in aluminum water bottles as a poisonous liquid can form!) All properly used treatments with iodine kill the cyst forms of giardia and amebae.

Chlorine tablets or drops can be used to treat water. The chlorine must be fresh and must be stored and used properly. Use 10 drops of chlorine bleach per quart or liter of water, rinse the cap threads with the mixture and let stand 30 minutes before use. This is not effective against the cysts of giardia or amebae, and therefore is not a recommended routine treatment for water.

Halazone is a chloramine used to treat water, but is not recommended as it has a shelf life of about 6 months and is usually not dated. Also, it is considered ineffective within a month after the bottle seal is broken. Cysts of giardia and amebae are not always killed by halazone use.

Water can be disinfected using a very strong dose of chlorine, which is then removed with an oxidizing agent before drinking. It does not remove chemical contaminants, but does render water tasteless and clear. It kills worms, viruses, bacteria, fungi and protozoa, especially giardia. A moderately priced system is available from Sierra Water Purifier®.

Filtration

Katadyn Pocket Water Filter® removes giardia, bacteria, fungi, cysts and parasites larger than 0.2 microns. It clarifies as well as disinfects water, but does not remove minerals. It can filter a quart or liter of water in 1½ minutes, but is very expensive and somewhat heavy. Replacement ceramic filters are available.

Katadyn also makes a system for larger groups that filters 3 liters of water per minute by hand or foot operation. Katadyn® KFT Expedition Filter is effective in the same means of water purification as the Pocket Water Filter. However, its cost and weight are great. Also, for large expeditions or basecamps, the Katadyn® TRK Drip Filter can purify up to 8 gallons of water in 24 hours. Water passively drips through a ceramic filter and is stored in a reservoir with attached spigot. Its cost is half that of the KFT Expedition Filter, it weighs less, and could be an ideal way to ensure quantities of pure water without the use of chemicals.

The First-Need® portable water purification device produces water meeting or exceeding U.S. Public Health bacteria standards without adding chemicals. It purifies by straining particles such as giardia cysts and parasitic tapeworms, debris, asbestos, and radio-active fallout. Also, it absorbs pesticides, herbicides, volatiles and organic contaminants. It can purify 1 quart of water in 1½ minutes, is moderately priced and light weight and the water it produces is clear and tasteless.

The First Need® Prefilter is a device that can be used to screen out coarse debris (10 microns or larger) from water before filtration. It is especially effective for glacial silt and prolongs the life of other filter canisters. The prefilter is inexpensive and lightweight.

The Water 1 Giardia Filter is a small, lightweight, lower priced filtration system with its own intake strainer to remove larger particulate matter. It can be operated by hand or foot. It has an estimated life of 3 years and includes a dye test kit to ensure the filter is working properly.

Water purification straws such as Pocket Purifier® are devices small enough to be carried in a pocket and are used to treat water bacteriologically and render it safe. The bottom of the device is placed in water, and water is drawn through the tube as one would use a straw. Filters and resins within the device kill bacteria and filter suspended particles and remove impurities to make the water palatable. They are relatively inexpensive and are lightweight.

Boiling

This is a very good way to render water safe to drink and is effective against cysts of giardia and amebae if boiled for an appropriate time. It is again important to note that boiling does not have residual protection against recontamination. The recommendation is to boil water for 10 minutes at sea level and one additional minute for each 300 meters (1,000 feet) above sea level. Although no chemical taste is added to the water, boiling does not remove the taste produced by minerals or organic material in the water. Boiling drinking water naturally requires additional fuel for the treatment process, over and above that required for cooking.

WASHING

Do not use any soap (even biodegradable) in bodies of water such as streams, lakes or catch basins. Even biodegradable detergents can cause chemical pollution of drinking water. Washing dishes with snow is quite effective, as snow is abrasive and removes most food; a rinse with a little hot water finishes the job. Fine sand from streams can also be used as an abrasive to remove foods from dishes, thereby avoiding the use of soaps. Always rinse in treated water and allow to air dry (dish towels and hands can recontaminate the dishes).

If biodegradable soap is used to wash dishes, clothes, or is used for bathing, use it in a pot of water 30 to 60 meters (100 to 200 feet) from the water source and above lake and river high water levels. Pour out soapy water in a small depression on soil that can filter out the soap and break it down. The best soil is vegetated and absorbs water slowly, presenting it to bacteria that decompose the soap. Too much soap in one area overtaxes the ability of any soil to degrade it. Soapy water should be disposed thinly over large areas, not continually in the same spot.

Provide a basin, soap and treated rinse water near the dining tent and another near the latrine area to encourage frequent hand washing. A waste water soakage pit should accompany each wash area to prevent waste water from collecting. A soakage pit is made by digging a 1 by 1 by 1 meter (3 by 3 by 3 foot) hole and filling it with small stones into which waste water is poured.

Obviously, bathing and washing dishes near the only water source can contaminate the water with soap. In addition, soap residues and food particles attract flies at the water source, which in turn can cause further health hazards.

Baking soda can be used as an excellent alternative to soaps. It is mildly abrasive and helps remove food particles from dishes. Also, it helps sweeten laundry and is very refreshing when used as a bath, and its impact on the environment is much less than even biodegradable soaps. Baking soda also is an excellent substitute for regular toothpaste. In all of its uses listed above, extra treated water for rinsing is not needed as baking soda leaves no residue after washing.

LATRINES

Burial of waste is important because human disease can be transferred through wastes; it is possible to carry dormant disease and be unaware of it. Wherever possible, use established facilities or latrines.

In areas where no exisiting facilities are available, construction of facilities depends upon the length of stay and the number of people in the group. Depth of the ground water must be considered and proximity to water sources must be studied before designating the latrine area. Although the cook or basecamp manager should supervise latrine construction and placement, actual maintenance should be performed by non-food handling personnel.

For individual use or single night stops in a lightly used area, a person can make a small hole, called a cat hole, taking care to dig down into the humus layer under the sod if possible and to cover after use.

For longer, but temporary stays, a trench latrine should be dug. Locate it on a hillside at least 100 meters (300 feet) from any stream, lake or marshy area so the waste will be filtered through the soil. Use the same distance from tents and cooking facilities. Make sure its drainage is AWAY from the water source, especially if the recommended distance is not feasible. Dig the trench into the organic humus layer under the sod if possible, because decomposers are active in the humus. The depth will vary from 12 to 36 inches, depending on the soil conditions, and an ideal width is 8 to 12 inches. Base the size of the trench on the number in the group and the length of stay. As a general rule, 2 feet of trench length should be provided to serve at least 8% of the number of people in the group at one time. Thus, for a group of 25 people, the trench should be 4 feet long (25 × .08 = 2; 2 × 2 = 4 feet).[3] Keep a specially marked spade by the latrine and spread a layer of dirt over the waste after each use. One spade should be provided for every 8 to 10 people.

For more permanent camps, a deep pit latrine should be constructed with the same placement considerations as for a trench latrine. It can be built 8 feet long and 12 to 18 inches wide. As a guide, depth should be 1 foot for each week of estimated use plus one foot of depth for dirt cover when it is to be closed. It is generally not desirable to dig deeper than 6 feet because the walls tend to cave in. Rock or high ground water levels may also limit the depth of the pit.[3] When only 1 foot of depth remains, cover in successive 3 inch depths of soil, compacting after each layer and mounding soil over the trench to a height of 1 foot.

Burn or carry out all paper articles used in the latrine. Do not leave them to rot or be strewn about by marauding animals. When possible, use toilet paper substitues such as snow, smooth stones or leaves.

In arid regions, there is very little humus, most of it existing under trees and bushes. Human wastes will not decompose in the predominantly inorganic, sandy earth of arid regions, but will only dissipate and filter through the ground following natural drainage routes. Make cat holes or latrines in areas remote from washes, waterpockets and streams. In warm areas, flies and odors become problems if waste is not carefully disposed.

In cold environments, flies are not attracted and odor is less, but decomposition is greatly slowed because of the low temperatures and lack of soil containing active decomposers. Because latrines made in and completely covered by snow can look like undisturbed areas after a few sunny days or a light snowfall, latrines should only be covered with a small amount of snow. Besides alerting an unsuspecting climber out collecting snow to melt for water, exposure of the waste facilitates decomposition. Such latrines should be made well away from camp on established routes.

In some heavily traveled routes in perpetual snow, local officials require climbers to place solid human waste in sealed plastic bags and carry it out for proper disposal.

In temperate regions, a good fly control program should be instituted including devices to cover the trenches between use and a semi-weekly use of powdered or spray insecticide in and around the trench.

GARBAGE DISPOSAL
Large amounts of leftover food should not be washed down a stream and left uncovered for animals to eat, as most prepared human foods are not good animal food sources. Always scrape remaining food from dishes and

carry it out, burn or bury it in the latrine, or bury it in a deep pit and cover with rocks or logs. Beside being unsightly, food left out to be eaten or to rot can attract insects and unwanted camp visitors, including ravens, which then tend to move on to other food supplies with a vengeance.

The controversy of "crevassing" garbage still rages. True, it is out of sight and will be pulverized by glacial action before it is ever seen again, but the possiblity exists that glacial runoff can be contaminated by this method of waste disposal. This is especially true as substances in crevasses are not exposed to most natural methods of decomposition, such as moderate temperatures and sunlight, and can remain trapped and frozen for long periods. Also, they ultimately run the risk of exposure at the terminus of the glacier.

TRANSPORTATION AND STORAGE OF FOOD

Food containers should be used only for that purpose and should not be used for products that could pollute the food (soaps, garbage or petroleum products). They should be air-tight and protected from sun, dust, insects and rodents.

Unopened tins of food should be inspected for swelling of one or both ends, leakage and severe structural bending. Any contents of such cans should be considered unsafe for consumption.

In most instances, refrigeration is not available and foods subject to spoilage above refrigeration temperatures (0° to 7°c. or 32° to 45°f.) should not be saved from one meal to the next. Meals should be carefully planned to provide for everyone, but with a minimum of leftovers.

In cold environments or above the snowline, the cold ambient temperatures or depressions in the snow can be used to keep foods cold, but such food should not be kept over 24 hours and must be guarded from sunlight which may raise the temperature of the food and cause spoilage.

RODENT AND INSECT CONTROL

In order to prevent contamination of food and utensils by rodents and insects, adequate measures must be taken. Proper food and utensil storage is the best prevention, but in certain instances, insecticides, pesticides and traps must be used. Besides fouling and scattering food, insects and rodents can transmit disease via contact with food, water and utensils.

REFERENCES

1. E. Peters, *Mountaineering: The Freedom of the Hills* 4th ed., Seattle: The Mountaineers, 1982: p. 59.
2. A.S. Evans and H.A. Feldman, *Bacterial Infections of Humans* New York: Plenum Medical Books Company, 1982: p. 16
3. Departments of the Army and Air Force, *Field Hygiene and Sanitation* Field Manual No. 21-10 and Air Force Manual No. 161- 10, Washington DC, 1970: pp. 38-39.
4. P.C. Beaver, R.C. Jung, and E.W. Cupp *Clinical Parasitology* 9th ed. Philadelphia: Lea and Febiger, 1984: pp.44-47.
5. A. D'Allessandro-Bacigalupo "Flagellate Protozoa" In: P.C. Beaver, R.C. Jung, eds. *Animal Agents and Vectors of Human Disease* 5th ed. Philadelphia: Lea and Febiger, 1985: pp. 13- 14.
6. R.G. Yaeger, "Amebae" In: P.C. Beaver and R.C. Jung, eds. *Animal Agents and Vectors of Human Disease* 5th ed. Philadelphia: Lea and Febiger, 1985: pp. 36-41.
7. G.H. Schwebach, *A Practical Guide to Microbial and Parasitic Diseases* Springfield, Illinois: Charles C. Thomas, Publisher, 1980: pp. 73-112.

Chapter 8

Baking at High Altitudes

"Know ye not that a little leaven leaveneth the whole lump?"
I Corinthians 5:6

*A*T HIGH ALTITUDE, water boils at a lower temperature and, therefore, foods cook more slowly. Leavening agents expand more, yeast doughs rise too rapidly and too high, sugar solutions become more concentrated in baking goods and frostings, and liquids evaporate faster in all cooking processes.

For baking cakes, yeast breads or quick breads, increase the oven temperature. Otherwise, walls of batter between air pockets formed by the leavening agents will not harden before the air pockets expand too much and rupture, releasing their trapped gas and allowing the cake to fall. (See accompanying illustration.)

For cakes, biscuits, muffins and quick breads, the amount of leavening must be reduced. Less air should be beaten into egg whites to prevent overexpansion of the air upon baking which results in the cake falling. Addition of more liquid offsets rapid evaporation that causes cakes to dry out. Buttermilk, sour cream and yogurt add needed moisture. Sugar amounts should be reduced because too much sugar causes a weak cell wall structure and a coarse and crumbly cake. The addition of one more egg than called for in the recipe will often convert a sea level recipe to a high altitude recipe. Usually, it is necessay to decrease butter or shortening because too high a concentration of fat weakens the cell structure and produces a tough cake. Self-rising flours should not be used because of the overexpansion of their leavening agents.

At high altitudes, yeast breads rise more rapidly and flavors do not develop as they should. Therefore, allowing the dough to rise once more than the recipe suggests can be helpful. Never let the dough rise more than double its bulk or air cells will collapse before they harden during baking and the bread will be flat and heavy. As a general rule, the baking temperature should be increased 25°F. for the first 10 minutes of baking time.

Deep fat fried batters such as doughnuts and fritters will be overbrowned on the outside and still raw on the inside unless adjustments in the recipe and fat temperature are made. The cooking oil temperature must be decreased to prevent the outside from cracking or burning before the inside is done.

LEAVENING AGENTS
Baking soda
Also known as as sodium bicarbonate, baking soda has no leavening action by itself and must be used in combination with an acid ingredient in the presence of water which causes the release of carbon dioxide and raises the dough.
Baking Powder
Baking powder is usually a blend of corn starch, bicarbonate of soda, sodium aluminum phosphate and calcium acid phosphate. It is a leavening agent that raises dough

by the production of carbon dioxide produced when the bicarbonate of soda (alkaline material) reacts with calcium acid phosphate or sodium aluminum phosphate (acid material) in the presence of water. There are three types of baking powder:

Double acting – (sodium aluminum phosphate and calcium acid phosphate). This reacts slowly in cold mixtures and releases most of its leavening during baking. It is best for high altitude use as it releases leavening in two stages, slowly, so the batter does not rise too rapidly. Substitute 1 teaspoon of double acting for 1½ teaspoon of any other kind of baking powder recommended in a recipe.

Tartrate – (combination of baking soda and cream of tartar or tartaric acid). It begins action at room temperature as soon as liquid is added. Dough must be mixed quickly and immediately placed in a preheated oven to bake before air escapes and the batter falls.

Phosphate – (calcium acid phosphate and/or sodium acid phosphate). This reacts slowly and produces the most leavening in cold dough.

Yeast

Yeast is an ascomycetous fungi that lives on sugars and reproduces by budding. Yeast causes dough to rise by the formation of tiny pockets of carbon dioxide released by the fermentation of the sugar. It can be dried in granules or can be compressed into cakes (refrigeration needed) for preservation and later use in baking.

Sourdough

Sourdough is a leavening agent of fermented dough containing live yeasts saved from one baking so that it can be used in the next, thus avoiding the need for fresh yeast. It can be purchased in packets to begin a "starter", or can be made from starches and yeast aged several days in water. Sourdough can be poured onto wax paper and dried in wafers for later use. (See recipe and instructions for sourdough starter at the end of Chapter 9.)

Steam

Steam is produced from water in batter and dough. During baking, steam is trapped in tiny pockets in the dough and acts as a leavening agent. As the dough sponge sets with further baking, the pastry holds its puffed shape, even after the steam is driven out of the pockets. Many pastries are produced with steam as the only leavening agent.

Air

Air that is beaten into a batter by vigorous mixing or air that is added to batter by folding in stiffly beaten egg whites expands when heated and causes the baked product to rise.

Setting the Sponge of a Cake

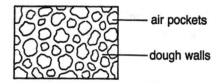

air pockets

dough walls

Optimal balance between strong dough walls and air spaces. It forms a sponge which "sets" as the product bakes and hardens.

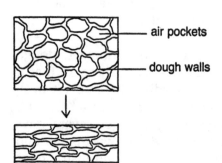

air pockets

dough walls

Too much leavening expansion causes thin walls in the sponge, which weaken and collapse, causing the cake to "fall".

INGREDIENT AND TEMPERATURE ADJUSTMENTS FOR HIGH ALTITUDE[1]

INGREDIENT	600-1,000m (2,000-3,500 ft)	1,000-1,500m (3,500-5,000 ft)	1,500-2,000m (5,000-6,500 ft)	2,000-2,500m (6,500-8,000 ft)
For each tsp of baking powder or soda, decrease by:	¼-⅓ tsp	⅓-½ tsp	½-⅔ tsp	⅔-¾ tsp
For each cup of sugar, decrease by:	1-1½ tbsp	1½-2½ tbsp	2½-3 tbsp	3-3½ tbsp
For each cup of liquid, increase by:	0-2 tbsp	2-3 tbsp	3-4 tbsp	4-6 tbsp
Increase flour by:	-	1 tbsp	2 tbsp	3 tbsp
Increase temperature by:	-	15-25°F.	15-25°F.	25°F.

Fill cake and muffin pans only one-half full, or they will overflow.

Over 3,000 meters (10,000 feet) use the chart for 2,000-2,500 meters and also add an extra egg or egg equivalent (reconstituted, uncooked powdered egg) and decrease butter or shortening by 1 tbsp per ½ cup.

1. B.M. Anderson and D.M. Hamilton, *The New High Altitude Cookbook* New York: Random House, 1980: p. 45.

Chapter 9

Recipes

"For humans, food has almost as much social utility as metabolic necessity. Carefully prepared meals are a lubricant for conversations, the formation of friendships, and are also psychologically satisfying."

COLORADO OUTWARD BOUND SCHOOL COOKBOOK

*T*HIS CHAPTER INCLUDES examples of dishes that can be made from common expedition foods. Recipes are written using familiar measurements found in most American recipes rather than metric measures. A list of abbreviations used in this chapter is included in Appendix I. Recipes used in pressure cookers are included in Chapter 10.

The general points listed below apply to most recipes:
- If a recipe calls for eggs, fresh eggs may be used if available, but an appropriate amount of reconstituted powdered egg may be substituted (NOT pre-cooked, freeze dried eggs).
- When a recipe calls for milk, either fresh milk, non-fat, dry milk reconstituted to the proper amount, or

canned evaporated milk diluted half with water may be used. Do not use sweetened condensed milk unless the recipe expressly calls for it.

- In many recipes, meats can be substituted for each other, such as beef patties substituted for sausage patties in spaghetti. Individual preference can be used to make these substitutions. Likewise, reconstituted forms of freeze dried tuna, ham, beef and chicken can be used instead of canned forms, and vice versa.

- Baked recipes were designed for a Coleman-type oven with thermostat, but reflector oven, pressure cooker, Dutch oven or slow skillet baking methods can be substituted where appropriate.

- When the word "reconstituted" appears in parentheses after an ingredient, it means that if fresh or canned products are not available, then freeze dried, dehydrated or low moisture products should be rehydrated according to package directions before use in the recipe.

- Recipes are designed in most cases to serve 6 to 8 people and may be doubled or divided, depending on group size.

- Using leftovers saves food, prevents disposal of food wastes into the ecosystem and spares fuel. Many recipes can be used for leftovers or suggest uses for leftovers.

- Some of the following recipes can be adapted to the pressure cooker. If so, sea level instructions are included at the bottom of the recipe. See page 150 of Chapter 10 to convert them to high altitude pressure cooker recipes.

- See Appendix IV for equivalents and substitutions that can be used in the following recipes.

- For some recipes, if an oven is not available, the dish can be heated SLOWLY over a very low flame. To help prevent burning, rotate the pan often and use a burner cover to help disperse heat and prevent scorching. This technique works best with dishes that only need to be heated thoroughly until bubbly. It is not suitable for baking.

Spaghetti with Clam Sauce

½ cup minced onion
¼ cup oil
1 6¼-ounce or 2 4oz cans chopped baby clams
½ cup non-fat, dry milk
3 tablespoons flour
1 package Hollandaise sauce mix
1 cup mushrooms (reconstituted; optional)
½ cup grated Parmesan or cheddar cheese
2 tablespoons parsley
1 teaspoon basil
¼ teaspoon pepper
2 tablespoons lemon juice
½ teaspoon dry mustard
¼ teaspoon salt

Saute onion in 2 tablespoons of the oil. Drain clams and reserve liquid. Add clams to sauted onions and set aside. Heat remaining oil and stir in the flour. Add enough water to the reserved clam liquid to make 2½ cups; stir in dry non-fat milk and gradually heat this mixture. Add flour mixture and Hollandaise sauce mix and cook over medium heat, stirring constantly until it thickens. Stir in all remaining ingredients and the clam mixture. Serve over one 8-ounce package of cooked spaghetti. Garnish with paprika or parsley. Canned shrimp or smoked baby oysters can be substituted for the clams.

Fried Rice

¼ cup oil
2½ cups uncooked rice
1 tablespoon minced garlic (reconstituted)
½ cup diced meat such as salami, corned beef, ham or sausage
½ cup chopped onion
3 beef bouillon cubes dissolved in ¼ cup boiling water
½ teaspoon pepper
1 tablespoon sweet bell pepper flakes
1 teaspoon ginger
1 teaspoon dry mustard
3 cups water

Heat oil in a large skillet. Saute onions and garlic. Add rice and meat and fry until the rice is dark golden brown. Add bouillon, seasonings and water. Cover and simmer until the rice is tender and the water is absorbed. Alternately, 7 cups of leftover cooked rice may be used and the water omitted.

Spanish Rice

2 cups uncooked rice
⅔ cup diced onion
¼ cup bell pepper flakes
4 tablespoons oil
½ cup tomato paste or reconstituted tomato powder
2 cups water
½ teaspoon pepper
2 tablespoons Worcestershire sauce
2 beef bouillon cubes dissolved in ¼ cup boiling water
1 teaspoon prepared mustard
2 teaspoons cumin
¼ teaspoon Tobasco sauce

Saute rice and vegetables in oil until slightly browned. Add remaining ingredients and bring to a boil. Cover and simmer on low heat until the liquid is absorbed and the rice is tender. If leftover cooked rice is available, use 6 cups of rice and omit the water. Stir frequently until the rice is hot and fluffy.

Fried Noodles

4 packages ramen noodles, crushed (save
   seasoning packet for other uses)
¼ cup oil
¾ cup water
1 teaspoon salt

Place all ingredients in a large non-stick skillet and simmer and stir until the noodles are soft. Increase heat and stir until the noodles are golden and crispy. Very good with vegetable or meat stir-fried dinners, as a topping for soups and with Oriental dishes.

This same recipe can be used with leftover noodles of any type. Drain the noodles well, omit water in the recipe and use as above. The seasoning packet out of the ramen package can be saved and used later to help flavor soups, gravies and sauces.

Potato Pancakes

3 cups grated or mashed potatoes (reconstituted)
4 eggs (reconstituted)
2 tablespoon flour
1½ teaspoons salt
¼ teaspoon pepper

Place all ingredients in a bowl and mix well. Place spoonfuls of the mixture in at least ¼-inch hot oil in a skillet. Fry on each side until golden. Drain well on toweling and serve hot. For extra flavor, add 2 tablespoons minced onion, 2 teaspoons dried parsley and ¼ teaspoon Tobasco sauce before frying.

Seafood Newburg

     2 tablespoons oil
     1 tablespoon each dried minced onion,
         parsley, bell pepper flakes
     1 cup mushrooms (reconstituted)
     2 tablespoons flour
     2 cups milk (reconstituted)
     ¼ teaspoon each salt, pepper, paprika,
         cayenne and nutmeg
     1 cup canned crabmeat, salmon, shrimp
         or tuna, drained
     ¼ cup sherry (optional)
     1 tablespoon lemon juice

Heat oil and add onion, parsley and bell pepper flakes.
Add flour and mix well. Stir in milk and wine and cook
until thickened, stirring constantly. Add spices, seafood
and mushrooms and heat thoroughly. Serve immediately
over rice, crackers or in crepes (page 123).

Ham Bake or Croquettes

     3 tablespoons oil
     4 6-ounce cans chopped ham
     1 cup dried bread or cracker crumbs
     2 tablespoons honey
    1½ teaspoons dry mustard
     ¼ cup water
     ½ cup diced onion
     1 teaspoon minced garlic
     ¼ teaspoon pepper

Saute onions and garlic in oil. Cool and mix with the
remaining ingredients. Form into a loaf, place in a shallow,
well-greased pan and bake at 350°F. until thoroughly hot.

For croquettes, the mixture can be formed into patties (1 x 4 inches) and browned on both sides in a skillet in a small amount of oil. Apple jelly, honey or pineapple chunks can be used as a glaze or garnish on the loaf.

Canned tuna or chicken can be substituted for the ham. Leftovers make good sandwich meat when placed between bread or pilot bread crackers. Left-overs from ham and chicken can be crumbled into soups.

Chicken Curry

  3 packages chicken flavored ramen
  3 cups boiling water
  ¼ cup diced onion
  1 teaspoon curry powder
  2 tablespoons oil
  2 packages instant cream of chicken soup
      mix
1½ cups milk (reconstituted)
  ½ teaspoon lemon juice
  2 6½-ounce cans diced chicken
  ½ cup prepared sour cream mix

Cook ramen noodles and seasoning packets in boiling water according to directions; drain. Saute the onion and curry in oil. Stir in the remaining ingredients and simmer until hot. Serve over the hot noodles. Two cups of tofu, cut into ¾" cubes and fried until brown in 4 tablespoons oil can be substituted for the chicken.

Skillet Pizza

2 cups baking mix (page 130)
⅔ cup water
2 tablespoons oil

Mix above ingredients and press into the bottom and sides of a well-greased 12-inch skillet. Pierce with a fork in several places. Bake 15 minutes at 400°F. Cool. Spread the crust with:

1 cup prepared spaghetti sauce mix
½ cup each onion slices or dices, green pepper, mushrooms, sausage or spiced meat slices (reconstituted)

Bake 30 minutes at 400°F., remove from oven and cover with 1 cup grated Parmesan or mozzarella cheese. Bake an additional 15 minutes.

Pizza

Crust:

2 cups flour
¼ cup warm water to which has been added 1 tablespoon dry yeast
¼ cup oil
½ teaspoon salt
½ cup warm water

Mix the ¼ cup warm water and yeast and let sit 5 to 10 minutes until foamy. Add the remaining ingredients and mix well. Knead the dough 10 minutes and let rise until doubled in bulk. Punch the dough down and roll out to fit the bottom and sides of an 8 by 8 inch square or a 10 inch round pan. Grease the pan well and place the dough in the pan.

Topping:
> 1 cup tomato sauce
> 1 package spaghetti seasoning mix
> 3 cloves garlic, minced
> ¼ cup green peppers, rehydrated
> ½ cup mushrooms, rehydrated
> ½ cup onions, sliced thinly
> 2 cups grated cheese

Spread the sauce over the dough and sprinkle with the spaghetti seasoning mix. Place the remaining ingredients evenly over the sauce and top with grated cheese. Bake at 450°F. until the crust is golden.

Mock Enchilada

> 3 large flour or corn tortillas (page 129)
> 2 cups chili (page 120), canned chili or
>   refried beans
> ½ cup each diced onion, diced green chili
>   peppers and diced tomato
> 1 cup shredded cheddar cheese or cheese
>   sauce made from powdered mix

In a 12-inch well-greased skillet place 1 tortilla. Cover with half of the chili, onion, peppers and tomato. Repeat these layers using another tortilla and the other half of the above ingredients. Place the third tortilla on top and cover with the cheese. Bake at 400°F. for 45 minutes or place over a VERY slow flame and heat until bubbly throughout.

Beef Croquettes

2 packages freeze dried Mexican or Denver omelette
1 cup dried and crumbled bread or cracker crumbs
4 packages crushed freeze dried beef patties
½ teaspoon salt
¼ teaspoon pepper
1 tablespoon steak or Worcestershire sauce

Place all ingredients in a bowl and add enough beef bouillon or water to soak and form a dough-like consistency. Form into patties (1 x 4 inches) and fry in a small amount of oil in a skillet until browned on both sides.

Excellent as a hot meat entree; prepared brown gravy or onion gravy mix can be served with them. Leftovers can be used as sandwich meat when placed between bread or crackers. Leftovers can also be crumbled into soups.

Dal Bhaat

2 cups pink lentils (mascar or masoor dal)
½ teaspoon turmeric
1 teaspoon ginger
1 tablespoon lemon juice
4 cups water
2 teaspoons salt
5 tablespoons oil
1 teaspoon cumin
¼ teaspoon cayenne
1 tablespoon minced garlic
1 teaspoon cardamom
½ teaspoon cinnamon
¼ teaspoon nutmeg

Wash lentils and drain. Place lentils, water, turmeric, ginger and salt in a large saucepan. Simmer until done. Add lemon juice to the cooked lentils and beat vigorously with a whisk to form a puree. Heat the oil and fry the cumin, remove from heat and add the cayenne, garlic, cardamom, cinnamon and nutmeg. Pour the seasoned oil over the lentil puree and stir. Serve over steamed rice.

Pressure cooker directions: 4 quart cooker, 15 pounds pressure, 5 minutes, let cooker cool gradually. Soak the lentils overnight according to the directions in Chapter 10. Make sure the cooker is only half full and that water covers the lentils. Cook the lentils, water, turmeric, ginger and salt in the pressure cooker, then proceed according to the usual directions in the recipe above.

Veggie Burgers

    2 cups soya mince
    ¼ cup diced onion
    1 tablespoon minced garlic
    1 tablespoon parsley
    1 teaspoon salt
    ¼ cup tomato paste
    ¼ cup sesame seeds or ½ cup finely
       chopped nuts
    enough water to make a stiff dough

Mix all ingredients well and let stand 1 hour. More water may have to be added. Using about 3 tablespoons of the dough, form patties ½ inch thick. Heat a small amount of oil in a frying pan and gently brown the burgers on both sides. Serve hot.

Macaroni and Cheese

1 16-ounce package elbow macaroni,
   cooked and drained
8 ounces grated cheddar cheese (reserve
   ¼ cup for topping)
2 cups water
⅛ cup oil
4 tablespoon flour
¼ teaspoon pepper
½ teaspoon salt
¼ teaspoon cayenne pepper
2 teaspoons dry mustard
¼ cup finely diced onion
⅔ cup non-fat, dry milk
½ cup crushed cracker or bread crumbs
½ teaspoon paprika

Place the oil in a saucepan and add the flour, mixing, to
form a thick paste; roll into a ball and set aside. Place
water, dry milk and all seasonings except paprika into the
saucepan and heat to scalding. Add small pieces of the
flour paste and stir constantly to thicken; cook slowly for
3 to 5 minutes. Add the cheese and stir until it is melted,
but do not boil the sauce. Pour over the cooked macaroni.
Sprinkle the top with the crumbs and the ¼ cup reserved
cheese. Garnish with paprika. If an oven is available,
bake at 375°F. for 20 minutes. Serve hot.

Fried Tofu

2 10.5 ounce packages tofu
1 cup flour or finely crushed cornflakes
½ cup soy sauce
oil for frying

Drain opened tofu for 30 minutes on toweling and discard
fluid. Slice crosswise into ½ inch thick slices. Roll in flour
or cornflakes. Place the breaded tofu in about ½ inch of
very hot oil in a skillet and fry until browned on each

side. Sprinkle 1 tablespoon of soy sauce on the first browned side while the second side is frying. Drain. Serve hot. Additional soy sauce, catsup, lemon juice, tahini, or other condiments may be served with the fried tofu. Also, spices such as parsley, garum masala, powdered soup mix or others can be added to the breading mixture for additional flavor.

Onion Rings

3 medium to large onions
2 cups prepared or left-over pancake batter
vegetable oil for frying

Cut onions into ½ inch rings and separate. In a skillet place 1 inch of oil and heat until it begins to smoke. Dip the onion rings into the batter and place gently in the hot oil; do not crowd. When brown, turn and brown on the second side. Remove from the oil, drain and serve hot.

Quiche

1 pie crust (page 137)
1 cup milk, scalded
1 cup rehydrated vegetables (potatoes,
    green beans, cabbage, peas, corn,
    carrots, celery, sweet bell pepper)
    best if mixed in combinations
½ cup diced onion
2 teaspoons minced garlic
4 eggs or equivalent in powdered eggs
1 cup cubed cheese
2 tablespoon oil

Saute the onion and garlic in the oil. Mix with all remaining ingredients and pour into the pie shell. Bake at 450°F. for 10 minutes, then at 350°F. for 30 minutes or until a knife inserted in the center comes out clean and the crust is golden. Allow to cool 10 minutes before serving.

Salmon Souffle

2 6½ ounce cans salmon
¼ cup diced onion
1 tablespoon minced garlic
¼ teaspoon pepper
¼ teaspoon cayenne
2 tablespoons dried parsley flakes
½ teaspoon dry mustard
2 eggs or equivalent in reconstituted powdered eggs
2 tablespoons flour
1 package Hollandaise sauce mix
2 tablespoons lemon juice

Mix all ingredients well. Grease a small loaf pan or a 9 x 9 inch square pan. With oiled hands, shape the mixture into an oblong loaf and place in the pan. Bake at 350°F. for 45 minutes, or until the loaf is browned on the surface and holds its shape well.

Chinese Chicken Rice Salad

¼ cup soy sauce
2 teaspoons prepared mustard
2 cups cooked, diced chicken
3 cups cooked, cooled rice
¼ cup minced onion
2 tablespoons bell pepper flakes, rehydrated
1 tablespoon oil
½ cup prepared Italian dressing
1 3-ounce can chow mein noodles

Blend the soy sauce, mustard and oil. Add chicken and stir to coat. Let stand 30 minutes to marinate. Stir in rice, vegetables and dressing. Top with noodles or place on a bed of noodles to serve.

Three Bean Salad

¼ cup diced onion
½ cup green beans
½ cup kidney beans
½ cup small white beans
¼ cup vegetable oil
2 tablespoons Italian dressing seasoning mix
2 tablespoons vinegar or lemon juice
1 teaspoon minced garlic

Cook the beans until done (may be cooked in a pressure cooker). Drain. Alternately, canned beans may be used, if available. Mix beans with all other ingredients and let marinate in a cold area 8 to 12 hours before serving.

Seafood Salad

2 4½-ounce cans shrimp, drained
3 cups cooked, cooled rice
½ cup diced onion
⅓ cup prepared Italian dressing
¼ cup ketchup or 1 tablespoon tomato
    paste plus ¼ cup water
1 tablespoon lemon juice
1 teaspoon dry mustard
1 teaspoon horseradish
¼ teaspoon salt
¼ teaspoon pepper
dash of cayenne pepper

Mix all ingredients well and let stand 30 minutes. Serve with pilot bread.

Vienna Sausage

Plain Vienna sausages in beef broth can be used in a variety of ways for quick meals or snacks:

1. Cold or heated from the can
2. Saute with steak sauce or barbecue sauce
3. Use in macaroni and cheese or bean dishes
4. Coat them with leftover mashed potatoes (2 cups potatoes mixed with 1 egg), roll in dried bread or cracker crumbs and brown in a skillet in 1 inch of hot oil for croquettes.
5. Spread them with prepared mustard, wrap in biscuit dough and bake until golden in a 400°F. oven.

Corned Beef Hash

1 12-ounce can corned beef, cubed
4 cups diced or hash brown potatoes (reconstituted)
1 cup grated cheese

Combine potatoes and corned beef in a skillet and simmer, stirring, until lightly browned. Sprinkle cheese over the top of the meat mixture and heat over a very low flame, covered, until the cheese is melted.

Meatballs in Onion Gravy

4 packages reconstituted freeze-dried meatballs
2 packages onion soup mix or 2 packages brown gravy mix plus ¼ cup diced onions
3 cups water
¼ cup flour mixed in 1 cup cold water

Prepare the soup mix as directed (or saute onions lightly in 1 tablespoon oil and add to prepared gravy mix). Add meatballs and water and simmer 10 minutes. Pour flour mixture into the meat mixture, stirring constantly until thickened. Cook another 5 minutes. May be served over rice, pasta or with mashed potatoes.

Tuna Casserole

½ cup diced onions (reconstituted)
2 tablespoons oil
4 6½-ounce cans tuna, not drained
3 cups flat egg noodles, uncooked
1 cup crushed crackers or dried bread
    crumbs
½ teaspoon pepper
¼ teaspoon paprika
¼ teaspoon salt
6 cups boiling water
1 package Hollandaise sauce mix or
    cheese sauce mix
1 cup grated cheese

Cook noodles in the boiling water and drain. Saute onions in oil in a large frying pan. Add tuna and seasonings. Stir in dry sauce mix. Add the tuna mixture to the drained noodles and stir gently to mix. Top with bread or cracker crumbs and cheese. Place in oven at 400°F. until the cheese is melted. Alternately, place the pan over a VERY low flame, covered, and heat slowly until the cheese is melted.

Lasagna

    2 cups water
    3 4-ounce packages freeze-dried sausage
        or beef patties (reconstituted)
    1 package spaghetti seasoning mix
    ½ can tomato paste
    1 12-ounce package flat egg noddles, cooked
    1 4-ounce package freeze-dried cottage
        cheese (reconstituted)
    1 cup grated Mozzarella or mild cheddar cheese
    ½ cup Parmesan cheese

Combine tomato paste, meat, spaghetti sauce mix and water and stir well. In a greased 10-inch skillet, place a layer of ½ of the tomato mixture, then ½ of the noodles, then ½ of the cottage cheese and ½ of the Mozzarella cheese. Repeat the layers and top with Parmesan cheese. Cover and bake at 400 °F. until thoroughly heated and cheese is melted. Alternately, cover and heat over a VERY low flame until bubbly. Serve with Parmesan cheese.

Leftover spaghetti sauce and noodles can be managed in this manner. Also, leftover beef, pork or sausage can be mixed to use in the meat sauce.

Chili

    2 packages freeze-dried beef patties or
        meat balls, crumbled
    1 quart water
    ½ can tomato paste
    1 cup diced onion
    4 tablespoons dried bell pepper flakes
    2 teaspoons minced garlic
    4 tablespoons chili powder
    1 teaspoon cumin
    2 tablespoons Worcestershire sauce
    1 teaspoon dry mustard
    2 tablespoons brown sugar or molasses

Mix all ingredients and simmer until thickened. If beans are available, they may be used in addition to the ingredients above, or can substitute the meat, if desired.

Pressure cooker directions: If dried beans are added to the recipe, soak 1 cup overnight according to instructions in Chapter 10. Use a 4 quart cooker, 15 pounds pressure, 45 minutes, reduce pressure gradually. If beans are used, fill cooker only half full and make sure liquid covers the beans.

Lentil Soup

- ¼ cup oil
- 2 tablespoons minced garlic
- 1 teaspoon cinnamon
- 1 cup chopped onion
- 1½ quarts water
- 2 cups lentils
- 2 cups diced carrots (reconstituted)
- 1 bay leaf
- 1 teaspoon salt
- ¼ teaspoon pepper

Clean and soak lentils overnight. Saute onions and garlic in oil. Add all remaining ingredients except salt and simmer until lentils are tender. Add salt at the end of the cooking time.

Pressure cooker directions: Soak the lentils overnight according to instructions in Chapter 10. Use a 4 quart cooker, 15 pounds pressure, 10 minutes, cool gradually. Make sure the cooker is only half full and that water covers the lentils.

Tomato Soup

    6 cups water
    ½ cup dehydrated potato flakes or powder
    ¼ cup diced onion
    1 tablespoon minced garlic
    1 tablespoon dried parsley
    3 beef or vegetable bouillon cubes
    1 cup tomato paste
    2 tablespoons oil
    ¼ teaspoon pepper
    ¼ teaspoon cayenne

Saute the onion and garlic in the oil. Add the remaining ingredients and bring to a boil, stirring so the dehydrated potatoes do not settle out and burn. Simmer 10 minutes and serve.

Onion Soup

    8 cups diced onions (reconstituted)
    8 beef bouillon cubes
    ¼ cup oil
    3 tablespoons minced garlic
    ¼ teaspoon pepper
    1 tablespoon parsley flakes
    1½ quarts water

Saute onions and garlic in oil until browned and clarified. Add the remaining ingredients and simmer until tender. Serve with grated Parmesan cheese for topping. Leftover rice or pasta can be added to the soup, as well as crumbled beef patties or meat balls for a more hearty soup.

Pressure cooker directions: 4 quart cooker, 15 pounds pressure, 5 minutes, cool cooker at once.

Crepes

    3 eggs (reconstituted)
    1 cup milk (reconstituted)
    ¾ cup flour
    ¼ teaspoon salt

Beat the eggs or mix powdered eggs until smooth. Stir in
the milk and beat well with a whisk or rotary hand egg
beater. In a small bowl mix the dry ingredients together,
add the egg mixture and beat well into a smooth batter.
Set in a cool place for 1 hour. Lightly oil a non-stick 8-
inch frying pan and heat over medium heat until a drop
of water sizzles and jumps around. Pour about 3 tablespoon of the batter into the pan and cook until the surface
looses its gloss and becomes dry. These can be stacked
up to six high on a plate after cooking. Use as a wrapper
for creamed meat and vegetable sauces or dessert sauces.

Hush Puppies

    1 cup cornmeal
    1 teaspoon baking powder
    ½ teaspoon salt
    2 to 3 tablespoons minced onion
    1 tablespoon bell pepper flakes
    1 egg (reconstituted)
    ½ cup milk (reconstituted)

Mix egg and milk and combine with dried ingredients.
Form into oblong shapes 2 x 4 x ¾ inches. Fry in 1 inch
of hot oil until golden. Drain on toweling and serve at
once.

Fritters

1½ cup complete pancake mix
4 eggs (reconstituted)

In a small bowl, beat ingredients together well. Drop by the spoonful into a skillet containing very hot 2-inch-deep oil. Fry on both sides until dark golden. Drain well on toweling.

For apple fritters, add ½ teaspoon cinnamon, ½ teaspoon nutmeg and 1 cup diced apples (reconstituted) to the batter before frying. For other variations, other fruits, spices, herbs and onions can be added to the batter before frying. Depending on the ingredients, they can be used for breakfast or as a bread accompaniment for dinner. For corn fritters, use 1 cup mashed kernel corn (rehydrated) in the batter.

Cheese Fritters

4 eggs or their equivalent in reconsti-
     tuted, powdered eggs
3 tablespoons oil
1 teaspoon salt
½ cup non-fat, dry milk
1 teaspoon baking powder
1 cup flour
1 teaspoon sugar
4 ounces firm cheese, cut into ½ inch
     cubes

Mix the first 7 ingredients to form a stiff dough. Using about 1 tablespoon of dough, surround a cube of cheese with a ¼ inch layer of dough, pressing it firmly to produce a good covering. Drop the fritters into 1 inch of hot oil and fry until golden on all sides. Drain on toweling and serve hot.

Dumplings

1 cup flour
2 teaspoons baking powder
½ teaspoon salt
½ cup milk (reconstituted)
1 egg (reconstituted)
8 cups broth, bouillon or soup stock

Mix dry ingredients and make a well in the center. Add beaten egg and a small amount of milk in the well and blend quickly. Add the rest of the milk and use as few strokes as necessary to blend all ingredients. Heat the stock to boiling in a deep, wide kettle with a close fitting lid. Drop the batter into the stock by rounded tablespoonfuls. Cover and cook for 20 minutes before lifting the lid. Test for doneness by inserting a toothpick in the center of the dumpling – it should come out clean. Remember not to overcrowd the pot and not to peek during cooking.

Raisin Scones

2 cups flour
½ cup raisins, dusted with flour
4 tablespoons brown sugar
1 teaspoon salt
1 teaspoon baking powder
¼ cup oil
2 tablespoons powdered egg
⅓ cup non-fat, dry milk
¾ cup water, to form a stiff dough

Place all dry ingredients in a bowl. Add oil and stir until the dry ingredients resemble corn meal and the oil is mixed in well. Add raisins. Form a well in the center and add the water, stirring only to moisten. Roll or pat out dough to ¾" thickness on a floured surface. Cut into 2 inch rounds or squares. Place closely together in a well-greased 9 x 9 inch pan. Bake at 400°F. until golden. Serve with butter, margarine, honey, or cheese.

Breadsticks

¼ cup warm water
1 tablespoon active dry yeast
2 cups flour
4 tablespoons oil
2 tablespoons grated Parmesan cheese
1 teaspoon salt
1 tablespoon non-fat, dry milk
½ cup water

Mix the yeast in the ¼ cup warm water and allow it to work 5 minutes or until foamy. Add all the remaining ingredients and mix well. Knead the dough 8 to 10 minutes until smooth. Place in a greased bowl, turn once and let sit in a warm area until doubled in bulk. Form the dough into sticks ¾ x 8 inches. Place ¼ inch apart on a well-greased sheet. Sprinkle with more Parmesan cheese or with 2 tablespoons spaghetti seasoning mix. Allow the dough to rest 15 minutes in a warm area. Bake at 350°F. until golden.

Cake Doughnuts

1 cup sugar
3 beaten eggs (reconstituted)
2½ tablespoons melted butter or oil
¾ cup milk (reconstituted)
3½ cups flour
4 teaspoons baking powder
1 teaspoon salt
½ teaspoon nutmeg
½ teaspoon cinnamon
¼ teaspoon mace

Add sugar to the eggs, then blend in butter and milk. Mix dry ingredients together then add them to the liquid and stir until blended. Heat the oil in a deep skillet to 350°F. The oil should be deep enough that the doughnuts can float. Roll out the dough ½ inch thick and cut with a doughnut cutter. Allow the cut doughnuts to sit and rest 15 minutes. Drop doughnuts into the oil and brown on one side. Fry only a few at a time to allow for floating room and so too much cold dough at one time does not decrease the temperature of the hot oil. Turn and brown on the second side. Remove and drain on toweling. Roll in powdered or granulated sugar mixed with cinnamon.

Raised Doughnuts

           1 tablespoon + 1 teaspoon active dry yeast
          ¼ cup warm water
           2 cups scalded milk (reconstituted)
          ½ cup shortening
           1 cup sugar
          ½ teaspoon salt
    4 to 4½ cups flour
           1 teaspoon cinnamon
           2 eggs, beaten

Mix yeast and water and set aside for 5 minutes. Add shortening to the hot milk and let cool. Add sugar, salt and yeast to cooled milk mixture. Add 3 cups of flour and mix well. Add enough remaining flour to form a soft dough. Knead 10 minutes. Place in a greased bowl, turn to coat and let rise until doubled in bulk. Punch down and add eggs, kneading until smooth. Cover and let rise again until doubled in bulk. Roll out ½ inch thick and cut with a doughnut cutter. Place on greased pans, cover and let rise until double. Fry in 2 inches of oil at 375°F. until brown on one side, turn and fry second side. Drain on toweling and roll in granulated or powdered sugar when cool.

Chinese Bread

Day 1 Place ½ cup flour and 1 cup of water in a glass or plastic container and add 1 teaspoon active dry yeast. Cover with a damp cloth and set in the sun 4 to 6 hours to produce a leavening agent.

Day 2 Use all of the starter from Day 1 and add enough water and flour to form a stiff dough. Place in a plastic or glass pan, cover with plastic and set in the sun until doubled in bulk. For every 2 cups of dough, knead in ¼ teaspoon soda and knead until the dough is extremely smooth. Save 1 cup of this dough as a starter for the next day. While kneading, salt, sugar or honey can be added to enhance the flavor.

For fried bread: Pinch off dough by the rounded tablespoonful and roll into a 6 to 7-inch round about ⅛ inch thick. Fry in a small amount of hot oil in a skillet on both sides until golden. Drain on toweling and serve immediately.

For steamed buns: Shape the dough into rounded tablespoonfuls. Place 1 inch of boiling water in a deep kettle and place a steamer rack above this so that water does not enter the steamer rack. Place the dough in the steamer rack with about ½ inch of space between pieces of dough. Cover and steam for 30-45 minutes until done.

For noodles: Roll the dough out thinly, cut into bite-size diamond shapes and place in boiling water or soup stock for 15 minutes, gently stirring occasionally to prevent sticking.

East Indian Puri

2½ cups whole wheat flour
1¼ teaspoon salt
½ cup softened butter
1⅓ cup plain yogurt

Cut the butter into the dry ingredients until crumbly and fine. Mix in the yogurt. Roll out to ⅛ inch thickness and cut with a 4-inch round cutter (a tuna can opened on both ends works well). Fry in 1 inch of hot oil in a deep skillet until brown and puffed on both sides.

Chapattis

    2 cups whole wheat flour or 1 cup whole
        wheat and 1 cup white flour
    1 teaspoon salt
    water to form a stiff dough

Knead the mixed ingredients well. The dough should not stick to the hands. After kneading 8 to 10 minutes, let the dough rest for 15 minutes. Break off walnut-sized pieces and roll out very thinly. Place in a hot, dry skillet, brown lightly on one side and turn. If the same dough is fried in a skillet with about ¼ inch of hot oil, it is called a paratha.

Tortillas

  1 to 1⅓ cup cold water
    1 teaspoon salt
    2 cups masa harina or 1½ lb. masa or 2
        cups flour
    1 teaspoon lemon or lime juice

Mix all ingredients together to form a stiff dough and knead 5-8 minutes. Let the dough rest for 20 minutes. Grease and preheat a skillet. Break off walnut size pieces of dough and roll out thinly. Fry in the skillet until the edges dry out; turn and cook until some color develops. Cool and stack.

Sopaipillas

1 tablespoon active dry yeast
¼ cup warm water
1½ cups milk (reconstituted)
3 tablespoons shortening
1½ teaspoon salt
2 tablespoons sugar
4 cups flour
1 cup whole wheat flour

In a large bowl combine yeast and warm water and stir; let it sit for 5 minutes until foamy. Add milk, melted shortening, salt and sugar and mix well. Stir in all of the whole wheat flour and 3 cups of all-purpose flour to form a sticky dough. Turn out onto a floured board and knead, adding flour until the dough is smooth. Place dough in a greased bowl, turn once to coat and let stand at room temperature until double in bulk. Knead dough on a floured surface to expel air. Roll out a portion of the dough to ⅛ inch thickness and cut into 3 x 4-inch rectangles. Place on a lightly floured surface and cover with a light cloth and let sit no more than 5 minutes. In a deep frying pan, heat 2 inches of oil to 350°F. Fry only a few sopaipillas at a time to prevent crowding. When the bread puffs and becomes pale golden, flip and fry on the other side. Drain on toweling and serve hot. Excellent served with honey and butter, or sprinkled with powdered sugar and cinnamon.

Baking Mix

⅓ cup shortening
4 cups flour (may be half all-purpose and
    half whole wheat)
8 teaspoons baking powder
1½ teaspoons salt
¼ cup non-fat, dry milk

Cut shortening into the dry ingredients until the consistency of corn meal. Store in a very cool place for 1 month in a covered container. If the temperature is too high, the mix will become rancid or will not rise properly.

Biscuits

2 cups baking mix (page 130)
¾ cup water

Combine the above ingredients and knead lightly on a floured surface to mix thoroughly. Roll out to ½ inch thickness and cut into rounds with a biscuit cutter or by cutting into 2 x 2-inch squares. Place close together on a greased pan and bake at 475°F. 15-20 minutes or until golden.

Yogurt

3¾ cups water
1⅓ cups non-fat, dry milk
1 tablespoon commercial powdered starter *(Lactobacillus bulgaricus* or *acidophilus)* OR ½ cup unpasteurized yogurt from a previous batch

Mix the water and powdered milk and scald in a 2 quart saucepan. Allow to cool to 40-43°C. (105- 110°F.) or until you can hold a finger in the liquid to the count of 10 and it still feels hot. Add the starter and stir well. During incubation, it is best to keep the temperature in the desired range, otherwise the culture will be killed at temperatures above 46°C. (115°F.) or will not grow below 32°C. (90°F.). The mixture can be placed immediately into a wide-mouth 1 quart thermos and incubated for up to 8 hours. Alternately, it can be wrapped in a down parka or sleeping bag and placed in a warm tent for 8 hours. Also, on a sunny day, the bowl can be covered with black plastic and placed in the sun 8 hours. It is best to make yogurt on a clear, sunny day, as the air temperature without radiation from the sun is too cold on cloudy days at high altitudes. Be sure not to jiggle, stir or otherwise disturb the yogurt while it is incubating, as it will cause separation of the yogurt. After the desired curd is set, stop the incubation by cooling the mixture. This can be accomplished by placing outside the tent in the shade, in a scooped out area of ice or snow or by placing the bowl in a cold stream. The length of the incubation determines the firmness of the curd and acidity (tartness) of the resulting yogurt. A soft curd is sweeter because less acid has been produced from the fermentation of the milk sugars. A firm curd is formed by greater amounts of acid production and the yogurt is much more tart.

Kefir

Follow the directions on page 131 for yogurt, only stop the incubation at the soft curd stage. Cool and sweeten with honey. If you have freeze dried strawberries or peaches available, or canned fruit such as blueberries, add ¼ cup of the fruit to 1¼ cup of kefir, stir well and drink.

Six Layer Bars

½ cup butter
1½ cups graham cracker or cookie crumbs
1 14-ounce can sweetened condensed milk
1 6-ounce package semi-sweet chocolate
    chips or ¾ cup chopped chocolate bar
1⅓ cup coconut
1 cup chopped nuts

Heat oven to 350°F. Place butter in a 9 x 9 pan and melt in the oven. Sprinkle graham or cookie crumbs over the butter and then pour the canned condensed milk evenly over the crumbs. Top with chocolate, coconut and nuts. Press down firmly and bake 25 to 30 minutes until lightly browned. Cool and cut into bars.

Peanut Butter Cookies

1 14-ounce can sweetened condensed milk
¾ cup peanut butter
2 cups baking mix (page 130)
1 teaspoon vanilla extract
granulated sugar in a shallow bowl or saucer

Preheat oven to 375°F. Mix milk and peanut butter until smooth. Add baking mix and vanilla and mix well. Shape into 1 inch balls and roll in sugar. Place 2 inches apart on a greased cookie sheet and flatten crosswise with a fork. Bake 8 to 10 minutes until lightly browned. Cool 1 minute before removing from the sheet.

Coconut Macaroons

5⅓ cups flaked coconut
1 14-ounce can sweetened condensed milk
2 teaspoons vanilla extract
1½ teaspoons almond extract

Preheat oven to 350°F. Mix all ingredients well and drop by rounded teaspoonfuls onto a well- greased baking sheet. Bake 8 to 10 minutes or until lightly browned. Immediately remove from the baking sheets.

For chocolate macaroons: Melt a 6-ounce package of chocolate chips or ¾ cup chopped semi-sweet chocolate bar in a saucepan. Remove from heat and fold in 2¾ cups flaked coconut, 2 cups graham cracker crumbs and 1 14-ounce can sweetened condensed milk. Proceed as above, baking 8 to 10 minutes.

Banana Cream Crunch

2 3½-ounce packages instant vanilla pud-
      ding mix
1 cup non-fat, dry milk
2½ cups water
1 cup prepared sour cream mix (without herbs!)
1 cup granola
1 cup banana chips

Combine pudding mix and dry milk in a bowl. Add water
and sour cream. Beat with a hand egg beater until smooth.
Place half of pudding in a serving bowl. Sprinkle half of
the granola and half of the banana chips over the pudding.
Top with the remaining pudding and granola and banana
chips. Two teaspoons banana extract may be added to the
pudding while mixing to enhance the banana flavor.

Oatmeal Date Bars

Crust:

2 cups oatmeal or quick-cooking oat cereal
½ cup baking mix (page 130) or complete
      pancake mix
1 teaspoon cinnamon
¼ cup sugar
1 cup melted butter

Filling:

1½ cups chopped dates (dried apriocots,
      prunes, raisins, figs, or other fruits
      can be substituted)
½ cup boiling water

Mix all crust ingredients into a stiff, dry dough. Divide
the dough in half. Press half of the dough into a greased
9 to 10 inch frying pan. Soak the fruit in the boiling water
for 10 minutes or until the water is absorbed. Spread over
the crust. Press out the remaining dough to fit over the

filling and press to the edges of the pan. Bake at 400°F. until the crust is golden or fry over VERY low heat on top of the stove, rotating the pan frequently to prevent burning.

Pudding Cake

6 6-inch leftover plain pancakes
1 package instant vanilla or chocolate
      pudding
⅔ cup non-fat, dry milk
2 cups cold water
1 teaspoon vanilla

Blend water, milk, vanilla and pudding mix until smooth. Alternate layers of pancakes and pudding in a 1 quart bowl. Allow to stand 1 hour before serving. The top may be garnished with granola, nuts, shaved chocolate or crumbled candy bars before serving.

Peach Melba Trifle

1 14-ounce can sweetened condensed milk
1¾ cups water
1 package instant vanilla pudding mix
2 cups whipped topping (page 143)
2 teaspoons orange extract
8 cups broken, stale bread or biscuit
      pieces
3½ cups peaches (reconstituted)
¼ cup raspberry or strawberry preserves

In a large bowl combine water and condensed milk and mix well. Add pudding mix and beat well. Set aside 5 minutes to thicken. Fold in whipped topping and orange extract. Place 4 cups of shredded bread in a 2 quart bowl. Top with half of the peaches, all of the preserves and half of the pudding mixture. Layer with remaining bread, peaches, and pudding. Serve immediately.

Orange Chiffon Pie

Crust:
   ⅓ cup melted butter
   1⅓ cups flaked coconut

Mix well and press into a 9-inch pie pan. Bake 15 to 20 minutes at 350°F. or until the edge is golden. Cool.

Filling:
   1 package instant vanilla pudding mix
   ¼ cup orange drink mix
   ⅔ cup non-fat, dry milk
   1¾ cups cold water

Place all ingredients in a bowl and mix well using a whisk or rotary hand beater until smooth. Pour into the cooled pie shell and chill or allow to sit for 15 minutes to set. Garnish with flaked, toasted coconut if desired.

Strawberry Banana Cream Pie

Crust:
   2 cups baking mix (page 130)
   ⅔ cup water
(may add 1 individual package hot egg nog mix for a richer crust)

Mix the above ingredients and roll out onto a floured board. Place in a 9-inch pie pan and prick sides and bottom of crust with a fork. Bake at 450°F. 15-20 minutes or until golden. Cool.

Filling:
   1 package instant vanilla pudding mix
   ⅔ cup non-fat, dry milk
   1¾ cups cold water
   2 teaspoons banana flavored extract

Blend above ingredients until smooth with a rotary hand beater or wire whisk and pour into the cooled pie crust. Allow to set 30 minutes until firm.

Topping:
   1 cup reconstituted strawberries
Place over pie filling. Slice and serve.

Pie Crust

   1¼ cups complete pancake mix
   ¼ teaspoon salt
   ¼ cup butter
   3 tablespoons water

Combine pancake mix and salt and cut butter into the mixture until it is the consistency of corn meal. Add water and stir until the dough forms a ball. Roll out on a floured board. Fit into a 9-inch pie pan, flute the edges and prick sides and bottom with a fork. Bake at 450°F. 15 to 20 minutes or until golden. Cool and fill.

Fruit Pie

   3 packages (2 servings each) of freeze
         dried apples or peaches (reconsti-
         tuted)
   1 package hot apple cider mix
   2 tablespoons flour or baking mix
   2 tablespoons melted butter

Mix all ingredients well. Place in an uncooked 9 inch pie shell and bake at 450°F. 40-45 minutes or until the crust is golden. If desired, a crumb topping can be prepared by blending ½ cup baking mix, ¼ cup brown or granulated sugar, 1 teaspoon cinnamon and ¼ cup butter and sprinkling this over the fruit before baking.

Shortcake I

   2 cups complete pancake mix
   ½ cup water

Mix together ingredients and roll out about ½ inch thick on a floured board (may use pancake mix instead of flour).

Cut into 3 x 3-inch squares or use a tuna can opened on both ends as a cutter. Place on a greased sheet and bake at 450°F. for 10 to 15 minutes or until dark golden. Split, spread with butter and serve with reconstituted fruit and whipped topping, yogurt or sweetened condensed milk.

Shortcake II

2⅓ cups baking mix (page 130)
1 tablespoon sugar
3 tablespoons melted butter
½ cup water
⅓ cup non-fat, dry milk

Mix all ingredients gently until dough forms. Proceed as above.

Quick Lemon Pudding

2 14-ounce cans sweetened condensed
    milk
¼ cup lemon juice

Mix the two ingredients together and allow to set 15 minutes. If desired, sprinkle top with crushed graham crackers, cookies or granola.

Spotty Dog Pudding

2 cups rice
4 cups water
1 cup raisins
1 can sweetened condensed milk

Cook the rice. Add condensed milk and raisins. This is excellent as a hot cereal for breakfast. Leftovers can be used in rice pudding.

Pressure cooker directions: See under Rice in Chapter 10.

Rice or Noodle Pudding

1 package instant vanilla pudding mix
2 cups water
⅔ cup non-fat, dry milk
1 teaspoon cinnamon
1 teaspoon vanilla extract
3 to 4 cups cooked rice or 4 cups cooked,
    drained noodles
¼ cup raisins

Blend the pudding mix, water, milk, cinnamon and vanilla well until no lumps remain. Add rice or noodles and raisins. Allow to set 30 minutes before serving. Garnish the top with cinnamon, if desired.

For bread pudding, substitute 4 cups dried, crumbled bread for the rice or noodles.

Chocolate Blackberry Torte

Crust:
    1½ cups baking mix (page 130)
    ½ cup sweetened condensed milk

Form a firm dough which resembles pie crust dough. Divide into 3 equal portions and roll out into 10-inch rounds on a floured board (baking mix can be used instead of flour). Heat 1 teaspoon of oil in a 10-inch skillet and fry the crust over low heat until firm and golden; turn and fry the second side.

Filling:
    1 package instant chocolate pudding mix
    ⅔ cup non-fat, dry milk
    1½ cups cold water

Mix these ingredients well until a thick, smooth pudding results.

Assemble by placing one crust on a plate and spreading it with half of the pudding. Cover with the second crust. Spread this with ½ cup blackberry jam. Place the third crust on top of the jam and spread with the remaining chocolate pudding.

Instant vanilla pudding made according to the directions above for the chocolate pudding can be substituted for the jam, and 1 tablespoon instant coffee can be added to the chocolate pudding for a vanilla-mocha torte.

Fruitcake

    1 cup whole wheat flour
    3 cups stewed, drained fruit (prunes,
        figs, apricots, dates, raisins)
    ⅓ cup honey
    ¼ cup oil
    1 teaspoon salt
    ¼ cup water or whisky
    ½ cup coarsely chopped nuts

Mix all ingredients well; batter will be thick. Place the dough in a well-greased 8 x 8 inch square pan. Bake at 300°F. for 1 hour. When cool, pour ¼ cup whisky over the cake. Wrap well in aluminum foil or a plastic bag and store 3 to 4 days before serving.

Fig Newtons

Crust:
    1½ cups whole wheat flour
    ½ cup melted butter or shortening
    ⅓ cup honey or syrup

Filling:
    2 cups diced dried figs
    ½ cup water

Simmer the figs in water 15 minutes and allow them to cool and soak up the remaining water. Mix the crust ingredients together and press into the bottom of an 8 x 8 inch greased pan. Spread the filling on top of the crust. Bake at 375°F. for 20 minutes. Cool, cut into squares and serve.

Blanc Mange

    1 quart water
    1⅓ cups non-fat, dry milk
    ¼ cup sugar
    1 teaspoon salt
    4 tablespoons cornstarch mixed with cold
        water OR 8 tablespoons flour mixed
        with 3 tablespoons oil
    2 teaspoons vanilla

Place all ingredients except the vanilla in a pan and heat slowly to boiling, stirring constantly. Cook 5 minutes. Remove from heat, cool and add vanilla. For a richer pudding, 3 tablespoons of powdered egg can be added before heating.

Garnish with granola or nutmeg, or use with fruits.

Orange Cappuccino Cake

    ½ cup orange drink crystals
    1 cup pancake mix (complete)
    4 tablespoons oil
    4 tablespoons flour
    1 cup water

Grease and flour a 9 x 9 inch pan. Mix all ingredients well and place in the prepared pan. Bake at 375°F. until done. Cool and split in half.

Icing:
    1 8 ounce plain chocolate bar
    3 tablespoons instant coffee
    ¼ cup butter

Melt the ingredients slowly over a low flame, stirring to prevent sticking. Spread the icing between the layers and on top of the cake.

Peach Crumb Cake

Cake:

>2 cups flour
>4 tablespoons powdered egg
>⅓ cup oil
>¼ cup brown sugar
>½ cup non-fat, dry milk
>1 teaspoon salt
>2 teaspoons baking powder
>1 teaspoon cinnamon
>¾ cup juice from drained canned peaches

Topping:

>2 14½ ounce cans peaches, drained
>1 teaspoon cinnamon
>½ cup brown sugar
>¼ cup melted butter or margarine
>¼ cup flour

Grease and flour a 9 x 9 inch pan. Mix all the cake ingredients until just moistened; pour into the prepared pan. Arrange peaches over the batter. Mix the remaining topping ingredients and sprinkle over the peaches and batter. Bake at 400°F. until done. Serve warm with whipped topping (page 143) or yogurt, (page 131).

Cheesecake

Crust:

>1 pie crust, baked (see page 137)

Filling:

>½ cup water
>¼ cup non-fat, dry milk
>8 ounces cheese, grated
>¼ cup instant vanilla pudding mix

Place grated cheese, dry milk and water in a sauce pan and heat until the cheese is melted, stirring often. Add the pudding mix and pour into the baked crust. Let cool. The cheesecake may be topped with fresh, canned or rehydrated fruit or grated chocolate.

Whipped Topping I

1 13-ounce can evaporated milk
3 tablespoons lemon juice

Whip with rotary hand beater until stiff peaks form. It will be increased in volume about 3 times.

Whipped Topping II

½ cup non-fat dry milk
⅓ cup cold water

Whip the above ingredients until peaks form. Add 1 tablespoon lemon juice and whip again until peaks form. Beat in lightly 3 tablespoons sugar.

Sourdough Starters

Commercial starters come in a dry, granular form. Follow package directions for use.

Homemade starter:
2 cups warm water
2 cups flour
1 tablespoon active dry yeast

Always use ceramic, glass or plastic containers and stir with a wooden or plastic spoon as the starter reacts with metal. Sprinkle the yeast over the water and stir. Beat in flour until smooth. Cover with a piece of porous cloth and set in a warm area at least 1 day or until it bubbles and has a sour odor. Stir at least once daily.

When only ¼ cup of the mixture remains after use, add 1 cup water and 1 cup flour, stir and let it sit overnight before use. If the starter has not been used and starts to die, discard all but ¼ cupful and add 1 cup of water and 1 cup flour, stir and let it work overnight.

Use 1 cup of active starter in place of each 1 cake or package of yeast and the dissolving liquid in recipes.

Chapter 10

The Pressure Cooker

*H*OW THEY WORK: Boiling of a liquid occurs when the pressure exerted by the vapor (steam) in a heated liquid becomes equal to the pressure of the surrounding air. Changing a liquid into vapor is called vaporization and involves the addition of heat. Continued application of heat does not make the liquid hotter, but merely makes it evaporate faster. (A liquid will not get hotter than its own boiling point.) Therefore, if air pressure is decreased, as occurs at high elevations, boiling will begin at a temperature lower than 100°C. (212°F.) because it takes less energy for steam to escape from the liquid. The cooking of food in open vessels becomes difficult under conditions of decreased air pressure because the food does not get as hot as it does at lower elevations.

For every 275 meter (900 foot) rise in elevation, atmospheric pressure is diminished one thirtieth of itself. Atmospheric pressure at sea level is about 760 millimeters of mercury (15 pounds/square inch or 29.92 inches of mercury). At 8,848 meters (29,028 feet), the summit of Mt. Everest, it is only about 240 millimeters of mercury, one third that of sea level.

Therefore, as atmospheric pressure decreases, the boiling point becomes lower. At 3,000 meters (10,000 feet), the boiling point is reduced to 90°c. (194°f.); at 5,000 meters (16,000 feet) it is reduced to 84°c. (183°f.); at 7,000 meters (20,000 feet) it is reduced to 80°c. (176°f.). As the boiling point decreases, the time required to cook foods by boiling increases. For every drop of 5°c. (10°f.) in boiling temperature, cooking time is approximately doubled.

Thus, a pressure cooker is a most useful device for cooking at altitude. If a closed, sealed vessel is used, the pressure of the steam over the liquid can build up inside and thereby raise the boiling point and cook the foods at a higher temperature and faster rate than without the artificial buildup of pressure. At sea level, an additional 5, 10 or 15 pounds of pressure increases the temperature of a liquid and its steam to 109°c. (228°f.), 114°c. (238°f.), or 121°c. (250°f.), respectively. At these superheated temperatures, cooking time is decreased one third to one fourth of the normal time required. At high altitude, pressure cookers save fuel, help maintain vitamin content of foods and allow the impossible to be accomplished.

For pressure cooking at high altitudes, however, cooking time recommended for pressure cookers used at sea level should be increased 5% for every 300 meters (1,000 feet) above the first 600 meters (2,000 feet). Following this rule, and using a weight of 15 pounds, the time would be increased as follows:

900 meters (3,000 feet)	5%
1,500 meters (5,000 feet)	15%
2,000 meters (7,000 feet)	25%
2,500 meters (8,000 feet)	30%

TYPES OF PRESSURE COOKERS

Pressure cookers are made by several different companies and therefore come in a variety of sizes and pressure

Parts of the Pressure Cooker

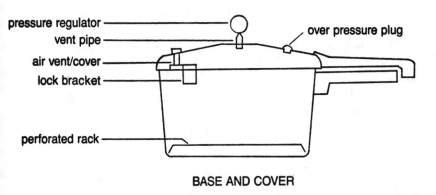

pressure regulator
vent pipe
air vent/cover
lock bracket
over pressure plug
perforated rack

BASE AND COVER

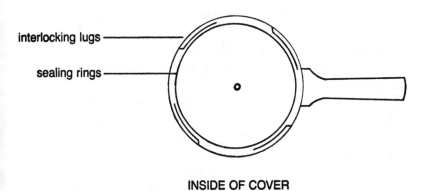

interlocking lugs
sealing rings

INSIDE OF COVER

choices. They are usually differentiated into family size (8 quarts or less) or canning sizes (greater than 12 quarts). The size chosen should be at least twice as large as the amount of dried beans or rice needed at one time to feed the group, to allow for expansion of such foods during cooking.

As a rule, sizes begin at 2.5 quarts and increase from 4, 6, 8, 12, 16 to 22 quart sizes. Most pressure cookers come with the capacity to cook at three different pressures: 5, 10 and 15 pounds. Some cookers, however, have only one weight available. It is advisable to obtain a cooker with three pressure adjustments to increase the pot's versatility.

General Rules for Using a Pressure Cooker

- Always read instructions and follow the manufacturer's suggestions for the unit.
- Food should never be allowed to come up so high in the pot so it will get into and block the steam vent pipe.
- Before each use, be sure the vent pipe is open. Hold the lid up to light to make sure it is open and clean with a pipe cleaner if it is clogged.
- With most foods, do not fill the cooker more than two thirds full.
- For beans, peas, lentils, rice and pasta, fill the pot only one-half full, as these foods expand, foam and froth greatly during cooking and can clog the pipe vent.
- When cooking dried vegetables such as beans, peas and lentils, cover the vegetables with water, add ½ cup oil and 1 tablespoon salt for every 2 cups of vegetables, let soak overnight, drain and then follow desired recipe. This cuts down on expansion and frothing during cooking.
- Higher pressures are necessary for fresh or dried vegetables and fruits, cereal grains, rice and pasta.

- High or medium pressures can be used with most meat, poultry and fish.
- Lower pressures are necessary for steaming breads and puddings.
- Do not cook pearl barley, apple sauce, cranberries or rhubarb in the cooker as they foam and can clog the vent pipe and lead to a dangerous situation with the cooker.
- Cooking time begins when the pressure regulator weight begins to rock gently. Adjust the heat to maintain a slow rocking motion.
- After cooking and the pressure has been completely reduced, remove the pressure regulator weight before opening the lid.
- On all newer models, a safety lock is present which keeps the lid locked in place until all pressure has been dissipated; only then can the lid be removed.

HOW TO DEPRESSURIZE THE COOKER

Pressure in the cooker may be decreased after the desired cooking time has been reached either immediately or slowly. As pressure is rapidly dissipated, there is intense boiling of the superheated liquid as the steam pressure on it is reduced. While many times this has no ill effect on the food, it is not recommended when dried vegetables, beans, rice, pasta and grains or large pieces of meat have been cooked. The activity of rapid depressurization causes beans to burst and disintegrate to mush, and changes the texture of meat. The pressure cooker recipes that follow designate whether to depressurize immediately or gradually.

To depressurize immediately either pour cold water over the pot until the hissing stops and the weight can be removed, or push the weighted pressure regulator slightly sideways until steam escapes. Allow this to continue until no more steam under pressure remains and the weight can be removed.

To allow gradual reduction of pressure, turn off the heat source and let the cooker cool until no more hissing occurs and the safety lock unfastens. Because of the gradual loss of pressure, the intense boiling produced with rapid depressurization is prevented.

CONVERTING TO PRESSURE COOKER USE

Standard recipes can be converted to pressure cooking by dividing the regular cooking time on the range or oven by 3, which gives the time necessary to cook at 15 pounds pressure. (Breads must always be cooked at 5 pounds pressure.) Recipes can be hastened from lower pressures, if desired, or if a recipe calls for a certain pressure, but your cooker has only one pressure setting, the following chart can be used to convert from one pressure to another. (If cooking at high altitude, be sure to increase the listed time according to the rule described on page 146.)

15 pounds	10 pounds	5 pounds
1 minute	1½ minutes	2 minutes
2	3	4
3	4	6
4	5	7
5	6	9
6	8	11
7	9	13
8	10	15
9	12	17
10	13	19
15	20	28
20	26	38
25	33	47
30	40	57
35	47	66
40	54	76
45	60	85
50	67	95
55	74	104
60	80	114

PRESSURE COOKER RECIPES

In addition to the recipes in this chapter, most instruction booklets that accompany the cookers include many recipes. Those recipes, and the ones that follow, assume that they will be prepared at sea level. Naturally, these can be adapted for higher altitude cooking according to the points covered previously in this chapter.

Several of the recipes in Chapter 9 can be adapted to the pressure cooker method. Those recipes have cooker size, weight recommendations, cooking times and cooling procedures listed at the end of the recipe.

A note on steamed breads: If the recipe calls for pressure to be applied, always cook at 5 pounds of pressure or less. If higher pressures are placed on the dough, the gas bubbles released by the leavening agent cannot overcome the pressure on top of the dough and it will not rise, resulting in a heavy, soggy mass. The bread must be baked inside a metal bread or cake pan or metal mold that can fit into the pressure cooker with at least ¾ inch of space all around and at least an inch between the top of the pan and the underside of the pressure cooker lid. Only fill the pan or mold ⅔ full. Since the shape of each pan used inside each size cooker differs, timing of the recipe must be adjusted accordingly. The larger the pan and amount of dough, the longer the cooking time. Also, recipes must be adjusted for longer cooking times at altitude. To check the bread for doneness, reduce pressure immediately at the end of the suggested cooking time, uncover the bread and insert a clean knife in the center. If it comes out clean, the bread is done. If not, cook 5 to 10 minutes more under 5 pounds pressure.

Basic Pressure Cooker Bread

4 quart cooker
no pressure

>   1 envelope dried yeast
> ¼ cup warm water
> ⅛ cup honey
>   1 tablespoon oil
> 1½ teaspoon salt
>   4 cups flour
>   1 cup lukewarm water

Add yeast to the ¼ cup warm water and let it stand 5 minutes until it foams. Add honey, oil and salt. Add the rest of the warm water and stir in flour cup by cup until the dough is firm, like a very stiff batter. Cover and set in a warm place until double in bulk; punch down. Place dough in a well greased pan and position it on top of the rack placed in the bottom of the cooker. Add 2½ cups hot water to the cooker. Put the cooker in a warm area and let the dough rise until the pan is ⅔ full. Lock on the lid and set over GENTLE heat. Do not use a weight on the vent pipe. When steam starts coming out of the vent, cook for 45 minutes. Open the lid and test the bread; cook longer if necessary. When done, invert to cool and remove from pan as soon as it is cool enough to handle.

Pressure Cooker Boston Brown Bread

4 quart cooker
5 pounds pressure

 2 beaten eggs or equivalent in reconstituted, uncooked powdered eggs
 2 tablespoons melted butter or vegetable oil
 ⅔ cup molasses
 1 teaspoon baking soda
 1 cup milk, reconstituted non-fat dry milk or diluted evaporated milk
 1 tablespoon vinegar or lemon juice
 1 cup flour
 1 teaspoon baking powder
 1 teaspoon salt
 2 cups whole wheat flour
 1 cup seedless raisins, lightly coated with flour

Beat together eggs and add melted butter, molasses, soda and milk. Sift dry ingredients in another bowl. Add the dry ingredients to the egg mixture and then add the vinegar while beating vigorously. Stir in the raisins. Pour into a well-greased pan until it is ⅔ full and cover tightly with aluminum foil. Place a rack in the pressure cooker and add 2½ cups hot wter. Stand the baking pan on the rack, lock on the lid but put no weight on it. Turn on and adjust heat so that a small, continuous amount of steam exits the vent for 30 minutes. Then place the 5-pound weight on the vent pipe and bring up to pressure for 30 minutes. Reduce pressure immediately and test for doneness. Cook longer under 5 pounds pressure if necessary. When done, cool in an inverted position and remove bread as soon as pan is cool enough to handle.

Excellent served sliced with cream cheese, cheese or peanut butter. It is a perfect accompaniment with baked bean dishes.

Pressure Cooker Nut Bread

4 quart cooker
5 pounds pressure

>   1 beaten egg or equivalent in reconsti-
>   tuted, uncooked powdered egg
>   ½ cup sugar
>   2½ cups flour
>   2 teaspoons baking powder
>   1 teaspoon salt
>   1 cup milk, reconstituted non-fat dry milk
>   or diluted evaporated milk
>   1 cup chopped walnuts or pecans

Beat together egg and sugar. Mix dry ingredients in a large bowl. Alternately add milk and dry ingredients to the egg mixture and beat until smooth. Stir in nuts. Fill a well-greased bread pan ⅔ full and cover tightly with aluminum foil. Place rack in pressure cooker and add 2½ cups hot water. Stand baking pan on the rack, lock on lid but put no weight on it. Adjust heat until a small stream of steam blows through the vent pipe and steam 30 minutes. Place the 5-pound weight on and cook for 30 minutes more. Reduce pressure immediately and test bread for doneness. Steam under 5 pounds pressure longer if necessary. When done, cool inverted on a rack and remove from pan as soon as pan is cool enough to handle.

For fruit-nut bread, add ½ cup finely chopped dates, apricots, raisins, apples or mixed fruits (lightly floured) when nuts are added.

Pressure Cooker Rice

4 quart cooker
15 pounds pressure

3 cups rice
6 cups water
2 tablespoons butter or vegetable oil

Place all ingredients in the cooker and lock cover in place. Set the 15-pound weight on the vent pipe and bring up to pressure. Cook 5 minutes and let pressure reduce on its own. Open the cooker and fluff the rice with a fork before serving. Yields 9 cups of rice.

• DO NOT FILL COOKER MORE THAN HALF FULL •

Pressure Cooker Beans

4 quart cooker
15 pounds pressure

2 cups dried beans
1 tablespoon vegetable oil
½ cup rehydrated or canned bacon or
    ham, diced
4 tablespoons brown sugar or molasses
1 teaspoon salt
1 tablespoon vinegar or lemon juice
1 teaspoon dried mustard
1 diced onion or ¼ cup dried minced onion
3 diced garlic cloves
2 tablespoons tomato paste or reconsti-
    tuted tomato powder
2 tablespoons dried sweet bell pepper
    flakes
water to completely cover the beans

Soak beans overnight and drain as described earlier in this chapter under GENERAL RULES. Heat the cooker and saute onions, garlic and meat in the oil until the onions begin to brown. Add remaining ingredients and water and stir. Place cover on cooker, lock and place the 15-pound weight over the vent pipe. Bring up to pressure and cook 45 minutes. Let the pressure drop gradually. Yields 4 to 6 servings.

For additional flavor, add 1 bay leaf, ¼ teaspoon ground cloves and ½ teaspoon cinnamon to ingredients before cooking.

● DO NOT FILL COOKER MORE THAN HALF FULL ●

Hot Potato Salad

4 quart cooker
15 pounds pressure

    1 tablespoon vegetable oil
    6 slices of bacon or ½ cup diced canned
        or reconstituted freeze dried ham
    4 cups potatoes diced or an equivalent
        amount of reconstituted diced freeze
        dried or dehydrated potatoes
    1 diced onion or ¼ cup dried, minced
        onion
    1 tablespoons sugar
    2 teaspoons salt
    ¼ teaspoon pepper
    1 teaspoon dry mustard
    ¼ cup vinegar
    ¼ cup water
    2 tablespoons minced, dried parsley

Saute onion and meat in oil in the heated cooker. Add the remaining ingredients and stir well. Close cover and place 15-pound weight on the pipe vent. Bring up to pressure and cook 5 minutes. Cool the cooker immediately. Serve hot. Yields 4- 6 servings.

This recipe can be cooled or leftovers can be combined with prepared mustard, mayonnaise, sour cream mix or yogurt, celery seed and crumbled scrambled egg as cold potato salad.

Pressure Cooker Stew

4 quart cooker
15 pounds pressure

>	2 cups reconstituted freeze dried beef patties or meat balls*
>	1 chopped onion or ¼ cup minced, dried onion
>	1 cup water
>	2 cups diced potatoes or equivalent reconstituted freeze dried or dehydrated potatoes
>	2 cups mixed, reconstituted freeze dried vegetables or fresh vegetables
>	½ can tomato paste (6 oz.) or equivalent amount of reconstituted tomato powder
>	1 tablespoon dried, minced parsley
>	¼ teaspoon pepper
>	1 tablespoon flour
>	¼ cup cold water

Place all but the last two ingredients in the cooker and stir. Close the cover and place the 15-pound weight on the vent pipe. Bring up to pressure and cook 5 minutes. Cool the cooker immediately. Make a paste of the last two ingredients and stir into the stew to thicken, simmering if necessary.

*Any available fresh or canned meats can be substituted in this recipe. If fresh meat is used, first saute it in 1 tablespoon oil and cook the meat separately for 5 minutes under 15 pounds pressure. Cool the cooker at once and continue recipe instructions above.

Pressure Cooker Fruit Crisp

4 quart cooker
15 pounds pressure

    ½ teaspoon dried orange peel
    2 tablespoons lemon juice
    4 teaspoons sugar
    1 teaspoon cornstarch or 2 tablespoon
        flour
    3½ cups rehydrated apples, peaches or
        apricots
    ½ cup packed brown sugar
    6 tablespoons flour
    1 cup rolled oats
    1 teaspoon cinnamon
    ¼ teaspoon salt
    4 tablespoons butter

In a well greased pan, mix the first five ingredients and set aside for 30 minutes. In a small bowl, mix butter and flour until the consistency of corn meal. Add the remaining ingredients and mix well. Sprinkle this mixture evenly over the fruit and cover tightly with aluminum foil. Place the rack and 2 cups of hot water in the cooker and set the pan on the rack. Place cover on cooker and lock. Put the 15-pound weight on the steam vent pipe and bring up to pressure. Cook 15 minutes. Cool the cooker immediately. Serve warm or cooled with whipped dessert topping, yogurt or milk. Yields 4 servings.

Pressure Cooker Brown Betty

4 quart cooker
15 pounds pressure

>   1 cup dry bread or cracker crumbs
>   ¼ cup sugar
>   1 tablespoon dried lemon peel or juice
>   and grated rind of one lemon
>   3 cups rehydrated apples, peaches or
>   apricots
>   ¼ cup melted butter
>   ½ teaspoon cinnamon

Combine bread crumbs, sugar, cinnamon and lemon in a bowl. Place alternate layers of the fruit and crumbs in a well- greased pan. Pour melted butter over the ingredients and cover the bowl tightly with aluminum foil. Set rack in cooker and cover with 2 cups of hot water. Place the pan on the rack. Cover and set the 15-pound weight on the vent pipe. Bring up to pressure and cook 15 minutes. Cool the cooker immediately. Serve warm with whipped dessert topping, yogurt or milk. Yields 4 servings.

Chapter 11

Spices, Condiments, Seasonings and Cooking Aids

*T*HE EASIEST WAY TO ADD variation, zest and palatability to foods is through the use of spices, condiments, and flavorings. This is especially true in camping and expedition situations where bulk, dried, and processed foods tend to be uniformly bland and uninteresting. The basic flavor of one food product can be ingeniously enhanced, varied, or altogether changed by the addition of flavoring. The addition of color, texture, and aroma to an otherwise ordinary dish can make an old standby a new delight.

The addition of spices to foods produces individuality and variation and is an expression of the art of cookery. Like any form of art, spicing foods must be studied and practiced, and can attest to the culinary talent and creativity of the cook. Although being adventurous is usually an asset, bold innovation with spices is usually a disaster. Most people have firmly established likes and dislikes of spices and their combinations, resulting from a lifetime of familiar uses of flavorings. Deviation from these established habits can cause unpalatability of the food, if for no other reason than unfamiliarity. Additionally, high altitude living seems to jade the palate and heavily spiced

foods do not appeal to most people, or can cause undesirable gastrointestinal effects. Therefore, spices are best
used in moderation and in established flavor patterns to
produce a well-complimented dish.

Because most spices and flavorings are used in very
small quantities, a well appointed spice rack is a light
weight, low bulk arsenal in the war against mundane
meals. The armamentarium of spices chosen should be
ones familiar to the cook and can also include commercial
seasoning mixes, if desired.

Although most spices can be obtained in several forms,
such as whole pods, seeds, barks, leaves, buds, cloves,
and bulbs, roots, berries, rinds, nuts, and portions of
flowers, the dried ground or powdered forms are easiest
to use, least bulky, and have stable flavor. Herbs are
easiest to use in dried, crushed form. Vegetable spices are
easiest to use in a dried, minced form, which also lends
color and texture to a dish. As an exception to the general
rule just mentioned, some spices may be used to their
best advantage in whole form, especially when used as a
garnish.

DEFINITIONS

Aromatic seeds – seeds of annual, biennial, or perennial
plants such as anise, caraway, coriander, and dill.

Essence – a substance that keeps, in concentrated form,
the flavor, fragrance, or other property of a plant or
food from which it is extracted, such as an essential oil.
Essential oils are volatile substances that give distinctive
odors and flavors to fruits and plants.

Extract – the flavoring obtained by treating a vegetable or
fruit product with alcohol and then evaporating the
preparation. Also used to denote a concentrated form,
whether solid, viscid, or liquid, of a food, such as beef
extract.

Condiment – a seasoning or relish for food, such as
mustard, horseradish, and pepper sauce.

Flavor bases and bouillon – compressed, powdered, or granulated mixtures of salt, vegetable proteins, animal fats, sugars, spices, monosodium glutamate, vegetable oil, and colorings used in various combinations to form a water soluble seasoning used as a clear broth or in gravies, sauces, and soup for flavoring.

Flavoring – an essence or extract added to a food or drink to give it a certain taste.

Garnish – a decoration of food that adds color or flavor.

Herbs – the leaves only of annual and perennial seed plants such as thyme, rosemary, basil, marjoram, and mint.

Marinade – a spiced pickling solution, especially a mixture of wine or vinegar, oil and spices in which meats, fish or vegetables are soaked, often before cooking.

Seasonings – generally are blends of spices and/or herbs such as bouquet garni, chili seasoning, poultry seasoning, and beau monde. Although salt is a chemical compound, it is considered a seasoning.

Spice – any of several vegetable substances used to season foods, adding interest, individuality, and piquancy. They are derived from bark, roots, fruits, or berries of plants.

HERBS AND SPICES

General points in the use of spices:

- To insure potency of flavor, keep herbs and spices in airtight containers and away from dampness. Plastic shaker tops can be obtained which fit over 35mm film canisters and make excellent durable, water-tight, lightweight spice jars.
- Ground spices release their flavor quickly, then diminish, so add them in the last half hour of cooking.
- If you have access to fresh herbs, use about twice as much as you would of the herb in dried form.

- Dried herbs may be crushed before use to enhance their flavor, or soaked in oil or wine, then drained before use.
- The function of herbs and spices is to bring out, not block out, the flavor of a food.
- In use, about ¼ teaspoon of dried herbs suffice for each 4 adult servings.
- One highly spiced dish per meal is best; more than one can confuse the palate.
- Restraint and selectivity in the use of unfamiliar, pungent or dominating spices is best.

The following chart lists suggested uses for herbs and spices. It is not all-inclusive and may differ from some personal tastes, but it can be used as a general guideline.

FOOD OR DISH	SPICES RECOMMENDED
Beverages – Hot	
Cider	allspice, cardamom, cinnamon, cloves
Nog	nutmeg, mace
Coffee	allspice, cardamom, cinnamon, mint, orange peel, vanilla
Tea	cardamom, cinnamon, cloves, orange and lemon peel, mint
Wines and rum	allspice, cardamom, cinnamon, cloves, orange peel, nutmeg
Beverages – Cold	
Tea	see Hot Tea
Fruit Drinks	anise, cinnamon, mint, orange and lemon peel
Vegetable drinks	basil, celery seed, black and cayenne pepper, mustard, thyme
Bean Dishes	see **Soups** – bean, pea, and lentil
Breads – Quick	
Biscuits, scones, breakfast and dessert loaves, cake doughnuts	allspice, anise, cardamom, cinnamon, cloves, coriander seed, nutmeg, mace, orange and lemon peel, vanilla
Breads – Yeast	
Raised doughnuts, pastry and coffee cakes	see **Quick Breads**

FOOD OR DISH	SPICES RECOMMENDED
Breads – Yeast	
Rolls and savory dinner breads	caraway seed, garlic, onion, poppyseed, sesame seed, parsley
Butter	dill weed, garlic, mint, onion, parsley
Cakes	
Dessert, tea, and coffee cakes	allspice, anise, cardamom, cinnamon, cloves, ginger, orange and lemon peel, mace, nutmeg, poppy seed, vanilla, coriander seed
Candy	ginger, sesame seed, anise, cinnamon, mint, vanilla
Carrots, cooked	allspice, caraway, cinnamon, ginger, orange and lemon peel, mace, nutmeg, parsley, pepper
Casseroles	celery seed, dill weed, garlic, mustard, onion, paprika, parsley, pepper
Cheese and cheese dishes	
Dips and spreads	caraway seed, chili powder, chives, dill weed and seed, garlic, mustard, onion, paprika, parsley, cayenne, sesame seeds
Quiche	basil, garlic, nutmeg, onion, parsley, pepper
Sauce	caraway seed, chili powder, chives, dill weed, garlic, mustard, nutmeg, paprika, pepper, cayenne
Souffle	onion, parsley, paprika, pepper
Chili	chili powder, cilantro, cumin, garlic, onion, parsley, pepper, cayenne
Chinese entrees	garlic, ginger, mustard, onion, pepper, sesame seed
Chocolate desserts and sauces	mace, mint, vanilla, cinnamon
Cookies	allspice, anise, cardamom, cinnamon, cloves, ginger, lemon and orange peel, mace, nutmeg, vanilla
Cream – iced and whipped	cardamom, ginger, mint, nutmeg, orange or lemon peel, vanilla
Custards	lemon peel, mace, nutmeg, vanilla

FOOD OR DISH	SPICES RECOMMENDED
Doughnuts	see **Quick and Yeast Breads**
Egg and egg dishes	
Deviled	celery seed, cumin, curry, dill weed, mustard, nutmeg, paprika, parsley, pepper, cayenne
Omelette	basil, chili powder, garlic, mustard, onion, parsley, pepper, cayenne
Scrambled	basil, chili powder, curry, cumin, mustard, onion, pepper, cayenne
Souffle	basil, cilantro, dill weed, garlic, marjoram, mustard, nutmeg, onion, paprika, pepper, parsley
Fish and Seafoods	basil, cilantro, curry, dill weed, lemon peel, marjoram, mustard, onion, paprika, parsley, cayenne, rosemary, sesame, tarragon, thyme
Fruits	
Fresh, rehydrated or canned	allspice, anise, cinnamon, cloves, ginger, lemon peel
Salads	anise, cinnamon, mint, allspice, ginger, lemon peel, poppyseed
Sauces	allspice, cinnamon, coriander seed, lemon peel, mint, nutmeg, vanilla
Garnishes (usually used as whole seeds or fresh sprigs)	celery seed, ground cinnamon, whole cloves, dill seed, mint, ground paprika, parsley, coarse ground pepper, poppy seeds, sesame seeds
Glazes for meat	cinnamon, cloves, ginger, orange and lemon peel, mint
Ham and cured pork	allspice, cloves, coriander seed, mustard, orange peel
Italian entrees	basil, garlic, marjoram, onion, oregano, parsley, pepper, rosemary, savory, thyme
Marinades for meats and vegetables	basil, bayleaf, caraway, cumin, dill seed and weed, garlic, lemon peel, mustard, onion, parsley, pepper, cayenne, tarragon, turmeric
Mayonnaise	curry

FOOD OR DISH	SPICES RECOMMENDED
Meats	
Beef	basil, bayleaf, curry, dill weed, garlic, marjoram, mustard, onion, paprika, parsley, pepper
Lamb	basil, bayleaf, curry, dill weed, garlic, marjoram, mustard, mint, onion, oregano, paprika, parsley, pepper, rosemary
Pork	basil, bayleaf, curry, dill weed, garlic, marjoram, mustard, onion, oregano, paprika, parsley, pepper, orange peel
Veal	basil, bayleaf, dill weed, garlic, marjoram, mustard, onion, paprika, parsley, pepper
Meatballs	garlic, ginger, mustard, onion, oregano, parsley, pepper, cayenne, sage
Meatloaf	cilantro, garlic, onion, oregano, parsley, pepper
Mexican and South American dishes	chili powder, cilantro, cumin, garlic, onion, pepper, cayenne
Pastas	caraway seed, celery seed, dill weed, parsley, pepper, poppy seed, sesame seed
Pies (fruit)	allspice, cardamom, cinnamon, cloves, ginger, lemon peel, mace, nutmeg
Poultry	basil, curry, marjoram, onion, oregano, parsley, paprika, pepper, rosemary, sage, savory, sesame, tarragon, thyme
Potatoes and potato dishes	
Boiled or baked	chives, dill weed, paprika, parsley, pepper
Creamed and soups	bayleaf, celery seed, chives, dill weed, garlic, mustard, onion, parsley, pepper, sage, savory, tarragon
Fried	garlic, onion, parsley, pepper, paprika
Scalloped	celery seed, dill weed, garlic, mustard, onion, parsley, pepper, paprika
Mashed or Whipped	chives, paprika, parsley, pepper
Sweet potatoes or yams	see **Pumpkin and Squash**

FOOD OR DISH	SPICES RECOMMENDED
Puddings	
Bread and rice	allspice, cinnamon, coriander seed, ginger, lemon peel, mace, nutmeg, vanilla
Chocolate	mace, mint, vanilla
Vanilla and tapioca	cinnamon, coriander seed, lemon peel, nutmeg, vanilla
Pumpkin and squash	allspice, cinnamon, cloves, ginger, mace, orange peel, nutmeg, pepper
Salads	
Fruit	see **Fruits**
Green leafy	garlic, onion, parsley, pepper, savory
Potato	caraway, celery seed, chives, dill seed and weed, garlic, lemon peel, mustard, onion, paprika, parsley, pepper, cayenne, poppy seed
Vegetable	basil, celery seed, chives, garlic, mustard, onion, oregano, parsley, pepper, savory, thyme
Sauces	
Barbecue	bayleaf, chili powder, garlic, lemon peel, onion, oregano, parsley, pepper, cayenne
Cream	bayleaf, chives, curry, mustard, nutmeg, onion, paprika, parsley, tarragon, white pepper
Dessert and fruit	cinnamon, ginger, lemon and orange peel, mace, mint, poppy seed
Tomato	basil, celery seed, garlic, marjoram, onion, oregano, parsley, pepper, cayenne
Sausage	cloves, garlic, onion, oregano, paprika, parsley, pepper, cayenne, sage, rosemary
Soups	
Bean, lentil and pea	allspice, bayleaf, cinnamon, cloves, coriander seed, garlic, onion, parsley, pepper, rosemary, savory
Vegetable	basil, bayleaf, celery seed, chives, garlic, marjoram, onion, parsley, pepper, rosemary, savory, tarragon, thyme, turmeric

FOOD OR DISH	SPICES RECOMMENDED
Squash	see **Pumpkin**
Stews	bayleaf, cayenne, rosemary, savory, tarragon, turmeric, basil, coriander seed, garlic, onion, oregano, parsley, pepper
Stuffing	garlic, marjoram, onion, oregano, parsley, pepper, rosemary, sage, savory, tarragon
Sweet potatoes and yams	see **Pumpkin**
Vegetables, cooked green	basil, cilantro, dill weed, marjoram, onion, parsley, pepper, savory, sesame seed, thyme
Yogurt	cinnamon, lemon peel, ginger, vanilla

CONDIMENTS

The following is a list of most common condiments. Individual preferences and familiarity with these and other condiments not included will help you decide which condiments to take along.

Catsup – the all-American favorite for flavoring eggs, potatoes, and meats. It can also be used in the preparation of chili, stews, soups, and tomato-based sauces.

Horseradish – a paste made of ground horseradish root, vinegar, vegetable oil, salt, and spices. A very pungent, sharp, hot condiment excellent when used in seafood and meat sauces.

Mayonnaise – a combination of oil and eggs, it is difficult to keep from spoiling after opening unless some form of refrigeration is available. Powdered mayonnaise substitutes are listed under Sauces in the food chart in Chapter 4.

Miso – fermented rice which is then mixed with soybeans, salt, and water. It is in a paste or powder form and can be used as a base for soup, stews, sauces, dips, and casseroles.

Prepared mustard – a paste made of mustard seeds, vinegar or wine, salt, and spices. Sometimes horseradish is added for zest or the mustard seeds used are hot. It is used in many ways, including sandwich spreads, potato salads, egg dishes, salad dressings, sauces for meats, and a dip for Oriental foods.

Salt (sodium chloride) – a chemical compound which lends a tang or piquancy and is used as a seasoning in most foods. It is also used in a highly saturated solution as brine for preserving and pickling foods. Salting meats and fish before cooking results in a loss of juices, and, therefore, vitamins. Do not salt the water for cooking beans and vegetables with skins as it toughens the skin.

Soy sauce – a condiment made of soybeans and wheat fermented and steeped in brine to form a dark, salty sauce. Used especially in Oriental dishes, but excellent as a meat marinade, in salad dressings, sauces, and gravies.

Tahini – a paste made from the pulp of sesame seeds. It is used as a dip for crackers and raw vegetables, for salad dressings, and is an essential ingredient for making hummus.

Tamari – fermented soybeans without wheat added. It is used like soy sauce.

Tobasco, chili, and hot pepper sauces – very hot, penetrating sauces used sparingly in many dishes to add zest. Excellent used in cheese and egg dishes, over cooked meats, in salad dressings, dips, soups, stews, gravies, and sauces for seafoods.

Worcestershire sauce – made from a base of anchovy, vinegar, catsup, and spices. Excellent when used in meats, sauces, stews, gravies, cold vegetable drinks, and salad dressings.

Vinegar – a sour liquid with a pungent odor, containing acetic acid which has been made by the fermentation of dilute alcoholic liquids such as cider, wine, or malt. It is used as a condiment and as a preservative in pickling. It is a 5% acid product. As a condiment, it is used in salad dressings, sweet and sour dishes, and over hot or cold vegetables.

EXTRACTS

These liquids are best in their pure, alcohol- containing forms, rather than imitation flavorings, although the former are more expensive. Most are used to flavor sweets such as cakes, cookies, candies, quick breads, pies, puddings, and custards. With a cache of your favorite flavorings along, plain vanilla pudding can be instantly enhanced or changed to another flavor by the addition of extracts. Hot and cold drinks can be "spiked" to add flavor variety, and basic sweet baked goods can be expanded into many diverse products. A list of commonly available extracts and imitation flavors follows:

Almond, anise, banana, black walnut, brandy, butter, cherry, chocolate, coconut, lemon, maple, Mapleine[R] (used with sugar to produce a maple-flavored syrup), orange, peppermint, pineapple, raspberry, rootbeer, rum, strawberry, and vanilla.

COMMMERCIAL SEASONINGS

Packets containing powdered bases for many seasonings and sauces are available in the supermarket and are perfect for adding variety or more flavor to many dishes without the use of individual spices, stocks, and thickeners. They are inexpensive, very convenient, and can prove indispensible in meal preparation. The following list gives examples of gravy, sauce, and seasoning mixes available:

Gravy – mushroom, chicken, pork, beef, turkey, brown, and cream.

Sauces and seasonings – white, curry, Hollandaise, Bearnaise, cheese, dill, spaghetti, sloppy joe, chili, taco, enchilada, beef stew, sweet and sour, stir fry, stroganoff, and sour cream.

THICKENERS

Corn Starch – a fine, powdery starch made from corn. Always mix with COLD water before using. After the cornstarch is mixed in water, it can be added to a hot liquid to thicken without forming lumps. Whereas flour forms a creamy-white gravy or sauce, sometimes with a bland, floury taste if too much is used, cornstarch forms a clearer, translucent, more glossy glaze to sauces, puddings, and gravies, and does not impart a flavor of its own. Add 1 tablespoon cornstarch for each 1 to 1¼ cup of liquid to thicken.

Flour – finely ground wheat. A paste of flour and cool water or flour and clear stock (cooled) in a ratio of 1 part flour to 2 parts liquid can be added to boiling liquids to thicken them. Vigorously shake the flour and cool liquid, and add slowly to the hot liquid, stirring constantly. Simmer 3 to 5 minutes after thickening to decrease the flavor of the raw flour. Use 2 tablespoons of flour for each cup of liquid to thicken.

Roux – a mixture of flour and fat used as a thickener for gravies and sauces. Two tablespoons of butter, margarine, shortening or oil are melted and an equal amount of flour is then stirred in. This mixture is used at a rate of 2 tablespoons per one cup of liquid to thicken. After thickening, simmer 3 to 5 minutes to cook the flour.

Arrowroot – a starch derived from the arrowroot plant. It produces a very delicate texture, but the sauce thickened with arrowroot should be served immediately. It thickens without boiling, so it is excellent for egg and cream sauces which should not boil. Use 2½ teaspoons of arrowroot to thicken 1 cup of liquid.

Tapioca powder – a starchy substance derived from the root of the cassava plant. It produces a very clear glaze and, like arrowroot, it should not be boiled. Substitute 1 tablespoon tapioca for each tablespoon flour for thickening. It is excellent when used to thicken baked fruit pies.

Baking mix – in a pinch, baking mixes can be used to thicken gravies and sauces. Flour is the thickening agent. Because a leavening agent is present, bubbles will form as the liquid thickens, but with simmering and stirring, the leavening properties are expended and the bubbles cease to form.

Gelatin – a substance derived from either vegetable or animal sources used to thicken liquids into a jelly-like state after cooling. Use 1 tablespoon unflavored gelatin to 2 cups of liquid.

Chapter 12

The Diet Survey

*I*N SOME INSTANCES, it may be desirous to maintain a very strict record of nutrition of foods eaten on an expedition. This is accomplished by performing a diet survey. After the types and amounts of food eaten per day are recorded, their values are obtained from the food package or from tables of food composition and are placed in chart form.

In using diet surveys, a record of the diet is essential. In addition to counting calories, other food components such as proteins, fats and carbohydrates can be calculated. A diet survey consists of the following:

- Record the type and amount of foods eaten per day for the duration of the study. Estimate the serving size of each food eaten (preferably in the same measure used in the tables of food composition). Include condiments, dressings, butter, sugar and salt. For prepared convenience items, often the calories and composition are listed on the package. The diet survey should be made on printed forms such as an individual nutrient intake chart (an example appears at the end of the chapter) and can be divided by food group or meals.

- Enter the composition of each food listed from the composition charts and tables.
- Add up total values for each food group or meal per day. These can later be transferred to master sheets for groups, time periods or other desired divisions.

In addition to supplying figures for each nutrient in the diet, the diet survey can be used to compute the proportion of calories coming from various nutrients. The number of calories derived from fats, carbohydrates and protein can be figured by multiplying the grams of each component eaten by the number of calories each gram of these nutrients supplies. Since each gram of protein and carbohydrate supplies 4 Kcal and each gram of fat supplies 9 Kcal, an example would be:

$$124 \text{ gms protein} \times 4 = 496 \text{ Kcal from protein}$$
$$150 \text{ gms fat} \times 9 = 1,359 \text{ Kcal from fat}$$
$$350 \text{ gms carbohydrate} \times 4 = 1,400 \text{ Kcal from carbohydrates}$$
$$3,255 \text{ Kcal TOTAL}$$

Then, the percentage of calories coming from each of the above nutrients can be found by dividing the number of calories by the total number of calories consumed:

$$496 \text{ Kcal protein} \div 3,255 = 15\% \text{ protein}$$
$$1,359 \text{ Kcal fat} \div 3,255 = 41\% \text{ fat}$$
$$1,400 \text{ Kcal carbohydrates} \div 3,255 = 43\% \text{ carbohydrates}$$

NUTRIENT INTAKE CHART

Food	Amount	Calories	Protein (gms)	Carbohy- drates (gms)	Total Fat (gms)	Unsatu- rated Fat (gms)	Satu- rated Fat (gms)	Choles- terol (mgs)	Minerals Ca Fe Na K	Vitamins A B C D K

Appendix I

Abbreviations

teaspoon	tsp or t
tablespoon	tbsp or T
ounce	oz
fluid ounce	fl oz
cup	C
pint	pt
quart	qt
gallon	gal
pound	lb or #
milligram	mg
gram	gm
kilogram	kg
liter	L
milliliter	ml
inch	in or "
foot	ft or '
degrees Centigrade	°c.
degrees Fahrenheit	°f.
calorie	cal (small calorie)
kilocalorie	Cal or Kcal (large calorie)
carbohydrate	CHO

Appendix II

Weights and Measures

is equivalent to:

1 tsp	⅓ tbsp
2 tbsp	1 fl oz
3 tsp	1 tbsp
4 tbsp	¼ cup or 2 fl oz
5 tbsp plus 1 tsp	⅓ cup
8 tbsp	½ cup or 4 fl oz
12 tbsp	¾ cup or 6 fl oz
16 tbsp	1 cup or 8 fl oz
2 cups	1 pt or 16 fl oz or 1 lb
4 cups	1 qt or 32 fl oz
2 pts	1 qt
4 qts	1 gal
8 qts	1 peck
4 pecks	1 bushel
16 oz	1 lb
100 lbs	1 hundredweight
2,000 lbs	1 ton
1 gm	1,000 milligrams
1 kg	1,000 gms
1 liter	1,000 milliliters
.946 liter	1 qt
3.79 liters	1 gal
.47 liters	1 pt
1 kg	2.2 lbs
1 ml	20 drops
4 ml	1 tsp
15 ml	1 tbsp
240 ml	1 cup
120 ml	½ cup
60 ml	¼ cup
454 gms	1 lb
28.4 gms	1 oz
1 gallon of water	8.33 lbs
°C	$(°F. - 32) \times \frac{5}{9}$
°F	$(\frac{9}{5} \times °C.) + 32$
1 Kcal	1,000 cal

Appendix III
Food Yield Chart

Food (uncooked)	Amount	Yield
apple	1 medium	1 cup sliced
apples (dried)	1 pound	6-8 cups rehydrated
apricots (dried)	1 pound	4½-5 cups rehydrated
barley	1 cup dry	3-4 cups cooked
beans (dry)	1 cup	2½ cups cooked
	1 pound	2½ cups dry
butter	2 cups	1 pound
cheese	¼ pound	1 cup shredded
coffee (ground)	1 pound	40-50 6-oz servings
coffee (freeze dried)	4 oz	50-60 6-oz servings
corn meal	1 cup	4 cups cooked
eggs (powdered)	1 pound	5¼ cups
eggs (powdered)	2½ tbsp egg + 2½ tbsp of water	1 whole egg
flour	1 pound	4½ cups
honey	1 pound	1⅓ cups
lentils	1 lb or 2¼ cups dry	5 cups cooked
macaroni	3-4 cups dry	1 pound
	1 cup dry	2-2¼ cups cooked
milk (non-fat, dry)	1 pound	5 quarts reconstituted
noodles	1 pound dry	6-8 cups cooked
	1 cup dry	1¼ cups cooked
oats (rolled)	2 cups dry	4 cups cooked
	1 pound	5⅓ cups cooked
peaches (dried)	1 pound	4-4½ cups rehydrated
potatoes	1 pound	2½ cups cooked
prunes (dried)	1 pound	3-3½ cups rehydrated
rice	1 cup or ½ lb uncooked	3 cups cooked
spaghetti	1 pound dry	5-6 cups cooked
sugar (granulated or packed brown)	1 pound	2¼ cups
sugar (powdered)	1 pound	3¾ cups
water	1 pound	1 pint or 2 cups

Appendix IV

Food Conversions

Food	Equivalent to:
1 tbsp corn starch	2 tbsp flour for thickening
1 tbsp flour	1 tbsp tapioca or ½ tbsp arrowroot for thickening
1 oz unsweetened baking chocolate	3 tbsp cocoa + 1 tbsp shortening or oil
1 cup fresh milk, whole	½ cup water + ½ cup canned evaporated milk
1 cup skim milk	1 cup water + 4 tbsp non-fat dry milk
1 cup canned evaporated milk	3 cups whipped
1 cup sour milk or butter-milk	1 cup sweet milk + 1 tbsp lemon juice or vinegar
2½ tbsp powdered egg + 2½ tbsp of water	1 egg
⅛ tsp garlic powder	1 garlic clove
1 tsp onion powder	¼ minced fresh onion
1 tbsp minced, dried onion	¼ minced fresh onion
1 bouillon cube	1 tbsp powdered gravy or sauce mix for seasoning

Appendix V

Can Sizes and Weights

Can Size	Net Weight	Volume	Cups
No. 1	10½-11 oz	9½ fl oz	1⅓
No. 1¼	14½ oz	12½ fl oz	1½
No. 1½	16 oz	15 fl oz	2
No. 2	1 lb 4 oz	1 pt 2 fl oz	2¼
No. 2½	1 lb 13 oz	1 pt 10 fl oz	3¼
No. 3	3 lb 2 oz	1 qt 14 fl oz	5¾
No. 5	3 lb 10 oz	1½ qt 4 fl oz	6½
No. 10	6 lb 9 oz	3 qts	13
No. 300	15½ oz	13½ fl oz	1¾
No. 303	16 oz	15 fl oz	2

Appendix VI

Food Company Addresses

Alpine Aire
P.O. Box 1600
Nevada City, California 95959
(916) 272-1971

All foods free of preservatives,
sugar, artificial flavors and
colors

Arrowhead Mills, Inc.
P.O. Box 2059
Hereford, Texas 79045
(806) 364-0730

No preservatives, additives,
pesticides or herbicides.
Distributed by local distributors
– addresses available from
Arrowhead Mills.

B & M Brown Bread
Pet, Incorporated
St. Louis, Missouri 63102

Bernard Fine Foods, Inc.
P.O. Box 487
222 South 24th Street
San Jose, California 95103
(800) 538-7941
In California (800) 662-6270

Chef-to-go
Division of Washington Trade
Corp.
5511 Sixth Avenue South
Seattle, Washington 98108
(800) 233-2074
In Washington (206) 767-2744

No preservatives.

Darigold, Inc.
Seattle, Washington 98119

Dri-Lite Foods, Inc.
1540 Charles Drive
Redding, California 96003
(916) 241-9280

Also distributed by Trail Foods
and Perma Pak

Familiar Foods, Inc.
City of Industry, California 91744

General Foods Corporation
White Plains, New York 10625

Hain Pure Food Company, Inc.
Los Angeles, California 90061

Morinaga Nutritional Foods, Inc.   No preservatives.
5800 South Eastern Avenue
Suite 270
Los Angeles, California 90040

Mountain House
Oregon Freeze Dried Foods, Inc.
770 West 29th Avenue
P.O. Box 1048
Albany, Oregon 97321
(503) 926-6001

The Pavo Company, Inc.   Distributors for many name-
3010 Niagara Lane   brand products as well as their
Minneapolis, Minnesota 55441   own line of foods.
(800) 328-3024

Perma Pak Distributors   Have their own line of foods.
2457 South Main Street   Distributors for Dri-Lite Foods.
Salt Lake City, Utah 84115
(801) 486-4159 or 4201

Red Wagon Store
Division of Boyd Coffee Company
19730 N.E. Sandy Boulevard
P.O. Box 20547
Portland, Oregon 97220
(800) 223-8211
In Oregon (503) 666-4561

Richmoor Corporation   Also carry Natural High foods
P.O. Box 8092   with no artificial ingredients or
Van Nuys, California 91409   preservatives.
(818) 787-2510

R.T. French Company
Potato Division
Idaho Falls, Idaho 83401

Smoky Canyon/Van Rich, Inc.   No preservatives in most
16850 Chicago Avenue   meals.
Lansing, Illinois 60438
(800) 323-3222
In Chicago (312) 474-7100

Stokely-Van Camp, Inc.
P.O. Box 9003
Chicago, Illinois 60604-9003

Stone Buhr Milling
Division of Arnold Foods
Company, Inc.
II Appletree Square, Suite 334
Bloomington, Minnesota 55420
(612) 854-0009

Stow-a-way Industries
P.O. Box 957
East Greenwich, Rhode Island
02818
(401) 885-6899

Have their own line of foods.
Also distributors for Mountain
House, Yurika, Dri-Lite,
Richmoor, and Smoky Canyon.

Survival Supply Company
15010 Keswick Street
Van Nuys, California 91405
(818) 902-0386

Distributor for Wee Pak, Smoky
Canyon, MRE's, Ready Reserve
Foods, and Alpine Aire.

Timbercrest Farms
4791 Dry Creek Road
Healdsburg, California 95448

Today Food Products
Portland, Oregon 97230

Trail Foods Company
P.O. Box 9309
North Hollywood, California
91609-1309
(818) 897-4370

Distributor for Mountain
House, Richmoor, Dri-Lite,
Smoky Canyon, and other
products.

Worthington Foods, Inc.
Worthington, Ohio 43085

Yurika Foods Corporation
33067 Industrial Road
Livonia, Michigan 48150
(313) 425-6300

No preservatives.

Appendix VII

Equipment Company Addresses

Champion Industries
35 East Poplar Street
Philadelphia, Pennsylvania 19123
(800) 523-4819
In Pennsylvania (215) 627-7477

Many Army/Navy surplus items and general camping equipment.

The Coleman Company
250 North St. Francis
Wichita, Kansas 67202
(316) 261-3211

Stoves, lanterns, coolers, jugs and vacuum bottles, heaters, propane and liquid fuel, canoes, rafts, air mattresses, tents, sleeping bags, and recreation supplies.

EPIgas International, Ltd.
Stockport, England

Four-in-one Water Systems, Co.
142 Lincoln Avenue
Suite 701
Santa Fe, New Mexico 87501

Sierra Water Purifier®

General Ecology, Inc.
151 Sheree Boulevard
Lionville, Pennsylvania 19353
(215) 363-7900

First Need® portable water purification device.

Katadyn Products, Inc.
Water Purification
CH-8304 Wallisellen
Switzerland

Katadyn Water Filter®

Mountain Safety Research
P.O. Box 3978
Terminal Station
Seattle, Washington 98124
(206) 624-8573

Stoves and accessories.

Nalgene Company
75 Panorama Creek Drive
Box 365
Rochester, New York 14602
(716) 586-8800

Plastic containers.

Optimus, Inc.
P.O. Box 1950
1100 Boston Avenue
Bridgeport, Connecticut 06601
(203) 333-0499

Stoves, lanterns and
accessories. Distributor for
Camping Gaz International®
and Sigg® products.

UltraLight
6089 Far Hills Avenue
Dayton, Ohio 45459
(513) 434-8010

Candle lanterns, fuel and
accessories.

Sport y's Shops
Batavia, Ohio
1 (800) LIFT-OFF

Carbon monoxide detector

Appendix VIII

Sample Menus

1. **Breakfast:**
   Scrambled eggs
   Freeze dried sausage patties
   Boston Brown Bread (page 153)

   Lunch:
   Tuna Casserole (page 119)
   Cheese Fritters (page 124)
   Fig Newtons (page 140)

   Dinner:
   Lasagne (page 120; use leftover sausage from
      breakfast)
   Breadsticks (page 126)
   Cheesecake (page 142)

2. **Breakfast:**
   Cake Doughnuts (page 126)
   Hot cereal

   Lunch:
   Onion Soup (page 122)
   Quiche (page 115)
   Peanut Butter Cookies (page 133)

   Dinner:
   Salmon Souffle (page 116)
   Vegetables
   Buttered noodles
   Peach Crumb Cake (page 142)

3. **Breakfast:**
    Fried canned bacon
    Pancakes
    Stewed fruit

    Lunch:
    Pizza (page 110)
    Three Bean Salad (page 117)
    Pudding Cake (page 135; use leftover pancakes
    from breakfast)

    Dinner:
    Spanish Rice (page 106)
    Mock Enchilada (page 111)
    Sopaipillas (page 130)
    Blanc Mange (page 141) or Quick Lemon Pudding
    (page 138)

4. **Breakfast:**
    Biscuits (page 131)
    Hot cereal
    Yogurt (page 131)

    Lunch:
    Seafood Salad (page 117)
    Crackers and sliced cheeses
    Fruit Shortcake (page 137) with Whipped topping
    (page 143)

    Dinner:
    Beef Croquettes (page 112) or Veggie Burgers (page 113)
    Hot Potato Salad (page 156)
    East Indian Puri (page 128; use leftover yogurt from
    breakfast)

5. **Breakfast:**
    Raisin Scones (page 125)
    Hash browned potatoes
    Omelettes

Lunch:
Ham Croquettes (page 108)
Buttered noodles
Onion Rings (page 115)
Fruitcake (page 140)

Dinner:
Dal Bhaat (page 112)
Plain rice (page 155)
Chapattis (page 129)
Six Layer Bars (page 132)

6. **Breakfast:**
Apple Fritters (page 124)
Hot cereal

Lunch:
Tomato Soup (page 122)
Grilled chapattis with cheese (use leftover chapattis
    from the previous evening)
Brown Betty (page 159)

Dinner:
Seafood Newburg (page 108) in Crepes (page 123)
Mashed potatoes
Rice Pudding (page 139; use leftover rice from
    previous evening)

7. **Breakfast:**
Potato Pancakes (page 107; use leftover potatoes
    from the previous evening)
Fried canned ham
Omelette

Lunch:
Beans (page 155)
Vienna Sausages (page 118)
Hush Puppies (page 123)
Oatmeal Date Bars (page 134)

Dinner:
Spaghetti with Clam Sauce (page 105)
Vegetables
Bread (page 152)
Orange Cappuccino Cake (page 141)

Suggested Reading

Adams, C.F. *Nutritive Value of American Foods*. U.S. Department of Agriculture. Agricultural Handbook No. 456. Agriculture Research Service. Washington, DC: U.S. Printing Office, 1975.

Adams, C.F., Richardson, M.*Nutritive Value of Foods*. U.S. Department of Agriculture. Home and Garden Bulletin No. 72. Washington DC: U.S. Government Printing Office, 1981.

Cogswell, B. *High Country Cooking in Colorado*. Memphis, Tennessee: Wimmer Brothers Fine Printing and Lithography, 1981.

DeGroot, R.A. *Pressure Cookery perfected*. New York: Summit Books, 1978.

Goldbeck, N., Goldbeck, D. *The Dieter's Companion*. New York: McGraw-Hill Book Company, 1975.

Hamilton, D.M., Nemiro, B.A. *The Complete Book of High Altitude Baking*. Chicago: Sage Books, 1970.

Krause, B. *Calorie Guide to Brand Names and Basic Foods*. New York: New American Library, Inc., 1984.

Pallister, N. *NOLS Cookery*. Emporia, Kansas: Emporia State Press, 1974.

Watt, B.K., Merrill, A. L. *Composition of Foods*. U.S. Department of Agriculture. Agricultural Handbook No. 8. Washington, DC: U.S. Government Printing Office, 1950.

About the Author

The author began her outdoor cooking experience as camp cook for fishing pack trips in the Teton Wilderness Area of Wyoming. Her love of mountaineering led her to Mt. Rainier in Washington where she cooked for two seasons at Camp Muir, at 10,000 feet, for clients and guides of Rainier Mountaineering, Inc. In 1984 she was the cook and basecamp manager for the successful 1984 China-Everest Expedition. In 1985, she held a similar position for the University of Colorado's Rio Abiseo National Park Research Project in Peru. Most recently, she was cook and basecamp manager for the 1987 International Alpine-Style Expedition to K2, in the Karakorums.

A veterinarian by profession, she lives in Telluride, Colorado, where she has a mobile veterinary practice and is a member of the Telluride Ski Patrol.

Notes

Notes

THE EXPEDITION COOKBOOK

Notes

THE EXPEDITION COOKBOOK